"More To Be Desired Than Gold"

A Collection of True Stories As Told By

J. Christy Wilson, Jr.

Compiled by Ivan S. Chow
Edited by Helen S. Mooradkanian

Copyright © 1992 J. Christy Wilson, Jr.

The cover picture portrays an Afghan riding on a donkey in northern Afghanistan as he directs the lead camel in a caravan in front of an old mosque outside the ruins of Balkh, one of the oldest cities in the world. The deep blue of the sky is the color of the semi-precious lapis lazuli stone which has been mined in Afghanistan since ancient times. Even excavations at Ur of the Chaldees, from which Abraham came, have unearthed jewelry of this blue stone which came from Afghanistan and which is set in gold. The title, *"MORE TO BE DESIRED THAN GOLD,"* thus contrasts the color in the same way with the deep blue sky. This picture was taken by James Cudney.

*Dedicated to
the Lord Jesus Christ
on
the occasion of the celebration
of the seventieth birthday
of
J. Christy Wilson, Jr.*

Contents

Foreword, *Billy Graham* . . . . *v*
Introduction, *J. Christy Wilson* . . . . *vi*
Preface, *Ivan Chow* . . . . *viii*

Chapter 1 The Greatest Prize
   "More To Be Desired Than Gold" 1
   Losing A Medal But Winning the Prize 4

Chapter 2 Muslim Friends
   "I Have Seen My Brother In Heaven!" 7
   A Muslim Priest Becomes A Beloved Physician 11
   "Father, Forgive Them ..." 12
   Send Their Voice to the Ends of the Earth 15
   The Language of the Heart 17
   A Medical Student Meets the Great Physician 18
   Only A Scrap of Paper 20
   The Itinerant Preacher Who Pulled Teeth 21
   The God Who Heals 23
   He Slipped In the Back Door 24
   Nationalism vs. Islam: The Thread That Unravels? 25
   The Moon Rock 29
   Seeing Is Believing 30
   "My Sins Are Forgiven" 31
   The Legacy 31
   Never Underestimate the Power of a Woman 32
   The Hidden Meaning of Numbers 32
   A Muslim Army Officer Comes to Christ 33
   When You Put Your Hand to the Plow 34

Chapter 3 The New Age Rage
   A "Missionary" Is Delivered of A Demon 37
   Startled By An Angel 41
   Escape From the New Age 44
   The Rich Young Sikh Who Followed Jesus 45
   The Tree Dwellers 50
   Doorways for Demons 51
   The 13th Floor and Other Superstitions 51
   The Demons Are Migrating North 53
   The Futility of Ancestor Worship 54
   Friday the Thirteenth 55
   The Hungry Fish 56

Chapter 4 The Collapse of Communism
The Courageous Pastor of Romania 57
Angels Guarding Beijing 59
A Communist Official Comes to Christ 60
The Day Communism Began To Crumble 62
Afghan Freedom Fighters. 65
We Don't Have To Tell Everything 68
From Tea Shop to National Leadership:Soong Dynasty 69
Billy Graham and Prevailing Prayer 70

Chapter 5 Today's Apostles
The Real John Birch 73
"I Want A God Who Answers Prayer" 76
Faith That Moves Mountains 77
Moody's Key to Revival: A Clean Slate 78
Pacific Islanders Lead Downed Pilot to Christ 79
A Monument in Gratitude for God's Word 80
David Livingstone in Africa. 80
The Beloved Amy Carmichael of India 82
The Little Girl Who Started World Vision 82
George Whitefield in New England 83
The Great Commission Was His Visa 84
Strange Birds Open Up Nepal 85
Revival Among the Zulus 86
Gregory and the First Christian Nation: Armenia 87
David du Plessis: "Mr. Pentecost" 88
A Trial Heard 'Round the World 89
Harold Ockenga Redeems the Time While Flying 91
Phone Books Help Complete Christ's Commission 91
Victory for Christ in the Comoro Islands 93
Attracted to Jesus in the Koran 94
The Blood of Martyrs 96
The Seminary That Goes TO the Students 101
God's Blessing on Christianity in Africa 102
John Eliot: Apostle To Native Americans 103
Samuel Zwemer: Apostle to Islam 105
Peter Zwemer: Mistaken for Jesus 107

Chapter 6 Personal Reminiscences
Lost In An Airplane Over Afghanistan 109
The "Hidden Highway" Into Afghanistan 113
Jesus Said, "I Will Build My Church" 121
Swimming To Afghanistan 123
"Sight" for the Blind 124
Silkworms, Trout, and Ducklings 127

Persecuted for the Sake of the Gospel 131
Accused of Spying in the Holy Land 132
The "Fully" Inspired Word 133
The Folly of Liberal Teachings 135
Liberalism Affects Student Missions 136
Kathryn Kuhlman 137
John Wimber 139
Worshiping As One People 142
An Antique Gun 143
The Prophecy 144
Three Types of Speaking in Tongues 144
"Are You Willing to Die For Me?" 146
The Billy Graham Telephone Ministry 147
An Evening With Billy and Ruth Graham 149
The Way Out 150
Operation Rescue 153
The Bible and Prayer in Public Schools 154
Families Praying Together and Staying Together 155
My Dad Said, "I See Jesus!" 156

Chapter 7 God At Work At Gordon-Conwell
From Bartender to Bible Translator 159
"He Knew Me Before I Was Born" 161
He Found Christ On the Assembly Line 162
Don't Close the Mission! 162
A Jew Finds His Messiah 163
Two Nurses in Calcutta 164
God's Blessings In African Missions 165
Setting the Captive Free 166
"Jesus Healed Me of an Incurable Disease" 167
Goodness And Mercy . . : 168

Chapter 8 Afghanistan's Apostle Paul
He Counted the Cost for Christ 169

Foreword by Billy Graham

Countless successful preachers of the Gospel have used illustrations to help listeners better understand and come to experience God's presence in their everyday lives. Today, stories of God's extraordinary work through ordinary individuals continue to encourage believers all around the world.

Here is a book loaded with experiences from real life which can help add fuel to the fire. Not only those who are expounders of the Scriptures, but those who are Christian workers, teachers, missionaries, evangelists, public speakers, youth counselors, and lay leaders can benefit from these illustrations of daily dependence on God's grace and power to minister effectively to people throughout the world, even in areas of different languages and cultures.

These stories serve to illustrate that the everyday experiences of Christians both at home and abroad are often stranger than fiction. Not only do we value the marvelous things the Bible says, but I think you will enjoy reading here in this book about the amazing things that the Living God does.

Billy Graham
Chairman of the Board of Trustees
Gordon-Conwell Theological Seminary

Introduction by J. Christy Wilson

This book of stories came into being as a complete surprise to me. Ivan Chow has been one of my students at Gordon-Conwell Theological Seminary. His grandfather was a dedicated pastor in China. According to Chinese custom, the seventieth birthday is the pinnacle of one's life. Therefore, Ivan and his wife Miang approached my wife and secretly obtained cassettes of my lectures over the past seven years.

Having been born in the Middle East and lived there much of my life, I have learned to teach and preach with stories. Our Lord Jesus Christ, along with revealing the Word of God, used many illustrations and stories to help His hearers better understand and remember the truths He taught.

Ivan and Miang took down seventy of the stories I had told and put them in a word processor and presented me with a laser-printed book in honor of my seventieth birthday. I especially want to thank them for their long hours of labor and love. I am also grateful to their children, Caroline and Jason, for allowing them time to do this.

When Dr. Robert Cooley, the President of Gordon-Conwell, saw this book which the Chows had prepared, he said he would like to have it published for distribution to the School's alumni/ae and others. I am grateful to him for all his interest and his help. This thus is a revision of the original.

Jim Cudney has been a long-time friend from Afghanistan who has a gift for taking beautiful pictures. He photographed the cover when he was in northern Afghanistan near the ruins of one of the oldest cities in the world, Balkh.

I am also deeply grateful to Helen Mooradkanian for graciously taking charge of the editing of this version. She is a professional editor who followed God's call to take her Master's at Fuller Seminary's School of World Mission, and was in charge of putting out the *Lausanne II Newsletter* for the Manila Congress in 1989. She has willingly used her talents to glorify God.

It also was very kind of Billy Graham, who is the Chair of the Board of Trustees of Gordon-Conwell, to agree to do the Foreword. I am also grateful to Allan Emery, Jr. for arranging for this to be done.

Thanks are extended to Gwyn Walters for his refreshing of my memory on the 1948 Olympics, to Dick Peace for his assistance in putting out the original copy, to Jack Lindberg for heading up this production, to Bob Dagley for arranging the printing, to Karen Caputo for seeing it through the press, to Wai-Yi Ma for the gifted graphics on the cover, to Susan O'Brien for wordprocessing, to Patricia Picardi for the formatting, to Paul Parisi for the final desktop publishing, to Jean Mills for proofing, to the Ockenga Institute Team of Bob Freeman, Sharon Carlson, Carole McLoughlin and Sara Mexcur for all their help, to Judy Kinney and Kevin Rall of the Media Department, to Lurline Mears and Mary Amirault as they worked with the President on this, to Judith Bynum for her help in the Book Centre, and finally to my dear wife, Betty for all of her constant support and patience.

For all these and the many others whose names are mentioned in this book, I want to express thanks for all your assistance. As the Bible says, "God is not unrighteous to forget your work and labor of love which you have shown toward His name" (Hebrews 6:10).

J. Christy Wilson, Jr.
Professor of World Evangelization
Gordon-Conwell Theological Seminary
South Hamilton, Massachusetts
April, 1992

(All the royalties on this book will go to the Cornerstone Foundation to help Gordon-Conwell students, especially internationals, with scholarships.)

Preface by Ivan S. Chow

It has been a great honor and privilege, over the past three years at Gordon-Conwell Theological Seminary, to have been an advisee of J. Christy Wilson, Jr. In so many ways, both directly and indirectly, he has been a mentor and a spiritual guide to me and my family.

These stories have provided both insight and inspiration for my own pilgrimage. To me they reflect the quality of the race Christy Wilson has been running for his Lord for most of his seventy earthly years.

In this his final year as Professor of World Evangelization at Gordon-Conwell, may these stories of Dr. Wilson be a testimony to the power of the Holy Spirit Who is at work in the lives of all who put their trust in the Lord Jesus Christ.

This collection is but a fraction of the hundreds of stories he has told on behalf of God's work in missions. Not all could be included. Not all were recorded. As Dr. Wilson himself would say: "Heaven alone will tell everything the Lord has done to and through His people."

To gather this collection of stories, under the limitations of a seminary student's budget, I am grateful for the help and support of the following:

The staff of the Ockenga Institute and the GCTS Media Center, and Dr. Richard Peace for the use of computers and printers;

The Sanders Christian Foundation, for the use of their recordings of Dr. Wilson's coursework (1985-1991);

Mrs. Betty Wilson, for taping her husband's courses at the Great Commission Theological Seminary in Los Angeles in 1991, and for checking and working the bugs out of the manuscript;

My wife, Miang, for assisting me in transferring the stories from audio to written form, and for her patience throughout the project.

Most of all, I thank the Lord Jesus Christ Who leads, empowers, encourages, and fills with joy unspeakable all those who call on His Name and take up their cross daily to follow Him. To Him be all glory and honor and praise.

Ivan S. Chow

Chapter 1

The Greatest Prize

"More To Be Desired Than Gold"

It was the opening day of the 1948 Summer Olympics in London, England, and the fanfare of trumpets announced the arrival of King George VI and the royal family.

The athletes were about to enter Wembley Stadium for the traditional parade of nations which would include marching past the King. No one watching could have ever suspected what was to take place later, behind the scenes. Yet a major event was in the making. Quietly and without fanfare. None of us would know its full impact for years, if ever. It would not be until several years later that I would receive a glimpse of it.

Yet it still amazes me.

Sitting up in the stadium, Gwyn Walters and I were caught up in the excitement. Gwyn was a fellow student from Wales (now Professor of Preaching at Gordon-Conwell). It was thrilling to see the athletes of each nation march past.

The delegation from Greece headed the parade since the Olympics originated there. Others followed in alphabetical order.

Then to my utter amazement came Afghanistan! I had no idea this isolated country would be participating in the Olympics. I felt a surge of excitement as I watched these unexpected contestants. But at the same time, I felt a heavy burden. How I longed to find some way to reach the Afghans with the Gospel! I prayed for them as they circled the stadium, prayed that I could reach them in some way while they were still here in London.

Even as a child growing up, I had sensed God calling me to go to Afghanistan as a missionary.

Now here I was an international student studying at the University of Edinburgh in Scotland and also at Cambridge in England, preparing to go to Afghanistan to teach English.

Earlier that summer, Gwyn and I had ridden bicycles in Wales to the places made famous by the great revival of 1904. We even met and talked with an elderly man who had been one of the young people in Evan Roberts' youth meeting, when the awakening first broke out. He gave us an eye-witness account of this great revival.

Yet all this paled as I looked forward to Afghanistan and the opportunity to teach and reach the people there for Christ.

My parents had been missionaries for twenty years in the city of Tabriz in northwestern Iran. As a little boy, I had often heard them praying for a land to the East, Afghanistan, where there were no Christians. Eventually, I felt God calling me to go there.

My mother told me that one time our Iranian evangelical pastor, the Rev. Stephan Khoubiar, asked me what I wanted to do when I grew up. I told him I wanted to be a missionary to Afghanistan.

"But missionaries are not allowed in Afghanistan!" he said.

"That's why I want to be a missionary there," I had replied.

And I had never doubted this calling.

After completing my studies in the States and working with Inter-Varsity for several years, I heard that the Afghanistan government had openings for teachers. Early in 1947, I filled out the forms and applied to their embassy in Washington, D.C. for a position teaching English. But I heard nothing for more than six months. It reminded me of Rudyard Kipling's statement, "Here lies the man who tried to rush the East."

And so, as an alternate plan, I decided to work on a Ph.D. in Islamics at the University of Edinburgh.

The day I sailed for Scotland on the *Queen Elizabeth*, a letter arrived at my parents' home asking me to go for an interview in Washington. The letter was forwarded to me in the British Isles.

I wrote back that although I was now enrolled for an advanced degree, I would be willing to set aside my studies if I had an opportunity to go to Afghanistan. They encouraged me to complete my degree and then reapply later.

And that's how I happened to be in London that momentous day.

Following the opening ceremonies, Gwyn Walters and I went to the British and Foreign Bible Society office near St. Paul's Cathedral and asked them if they had any New Testaments available in Persian. This was the closest language to the Dari dialect of Farsi in Afghanistan. They said they did.

We asked the Bible Society if they could possibly give a copy of the New Testament to each of the Afghan athletes since they had none available in their nation.

The Bible Society liked the idea very much. In fact, not only would they supply New Testaments to the Afghans in their own dialect, they said, but they would also provide New Testaments to all the Olympic athletes in their own language. And as an added bonus, they suggested stamping each New Testament with the five-circle Olympic symbol in gold.

At that time, there was no problem with security at the Olympic Village, and the Bible Society easily entered the Village and distributed the Scriptures without any difficulty.

Nothing more was heard about all this, until several years later.

Then one day, when I was teaching English in Kabul, Afghanistan, one of my students asked to see me privately. After class we went for a walk in the garden of the school. When we were alone, he told me that he had been reading a very interesting book and wanted to ask me some questions about it. He reached into the inner pocket of his coat and pulled out a New Testament in Farsi.

On the cover the Olympic seal was emblazoned in gold!

One of the Olympic athletes from Afghanistan had brought it back as a prized possession and had loaned it to this student. The Afghan contestants had not won any Olympic medals but they had received something far more precious—God's Word!

While I don't know what ultimately happened to that student, I do know the Lord planted the seed in his heart and He would continue to work in him.

As David says in Psalms, God's Word or the Scriptures are—

> *more to be desired than gold, yes than much fine gold; sweeter also than honey and the honeycomb ... And in keeping them there is great reward.*
>
> *(Psalm 19:10,11)*

There is more to be desired than Olympic gold!

Losing A Medal But Winning the Prize

While the Olympic gold is highly prized, there was one contest, some years prior to the 1948 Games, where the gold medal was not the most coveted prize.

I was a student at Princeton University at the time. One of our annual traditions was a one-mile relay race between classes. A wealthy alumnus donated gold medals each year to the winners. In that particular year, I was chosen to serve as the anchor on our class team. I knew that a competing class had Skip Payne running the last leg for his team. And Skip was faster than I was.

The race began, with our first three runners taking a slight lead. I received the baton a few feet ahead of Skip and ran as fast as I could. As we moved down the final stretch, I could hear him gaining ground on me. Surely he would pass me and break the tape at the finish line.

But Skip ran too close to me, and my right hand unwittingly hit his baton, knocking it to the ground. By the time he stopped to pick it up, I had crossed the finish line and had won the race.

I felt terrible about what had happened.

That night I went to Skip's dormitory room and offered him the gold medal. But he refused to take it.

Then I told him of an even greater race he could win if he received Jesus Christ as his personal Savior.

The Apostle Paul said, "Forgetting what is behind and reaching for that which is before, I press toward the mark for the prize of the high calling of God in Jesus Christ" (Philippians 3:13,14).

As we talked far into the night, I shared with Skip that we are all sinners—"*all* have sinned and have come short of the glory of God." But although "the wages of sin is death, the gift of God is eternal life through Jesus Christ our Lord."

Then we talked of God's amazing love, how He reaches out to us no matter who we are. "Skip," I said, "the Bible says 'God has shown His love for us in that while we were yet sinners, Christ died for us.'"

Skip was ready to receive all that the Lord had for him. When he asked the Lord to forgive him his sins, he knew God *did* forgive him because, as I went on to show him, "If we confess our sins, He is faithful and just to forgive our sins and to cleanse us from all unrighteousness."

That night Skip won a far greater prize than the gold medal! He bowed his head and asked Jesus to become his Savior and Lord.

In taking this step of faith, he realized he personally had to accept the Lord because the Scriptures say that "as many as receive Him, to them He gives the right to become the children of God."

The Apostle Peter also wrote that our faith is more precious than gold which perishes. We have not been purchased from our sins with silver and gold, but by the precious blood of Christ.

One day I look forward to seeing Skip again in heaven and hearing him say along with Paul, "I have finished the race, I have kept the faith. Now there is laid up for me a crown of righteousness which the Lord the Righteous Judge will give me at that Day" (II Timothy 4:7,8).

The Apostle Paul writes again in another letter to young Timothy: "Bodily training or exercise profits for a little while, but godliness is profitable in every way, having promise for this life and for the life to come" (I Timothy 4:8).

Like Skip Payne, many young people are discovering the riches of the world do not last. Neither do they satisfy. They are searching for the imperishable, which is *"more to be desired than gold."*

This book of stories tells of many others who found true riches and eternal satisfaction in Jesus Christ.

6 *"More To Be Desired Than Gold"*

Chapter 2

Muslim Friends

"I Have Seen My Brother In Heaven!"

Abraham was a young Afghan who came to the United States and was befriended by Christians who invited him to their home and their church. Before long he accepted Christ as his Savior. When he returned to Afghanistan, he told his friends that there was some truth in Islam but the whole truth was in Christ.

Immediately, his friends began to persecute him. They took away his Bible, tore it up and warned him that if he said another word about Christ, they would beat him up.

One night Abraham slipped into our home after dark and said, "Tomorrow I have been ordered to go on trial for my life before the leading judge in Kabul. They have charged me with the sin of becoming a Christian. What should I do?" I read Matthew 10:23 to him where Jesus said that if you are persecuted in one city, flee to the next.

"But," he replied, "when I arrived at the airport in Kabul, they took away my passport. How can I leave?"

"Why don't you join the Pashtun nomads who walk across the border and through the Khyber Pass with their camel caravans," I suggested. "Dress like one of them and you will not be recognized." So disguised in this way, Abraham safely crossed the border into Pakistan, where he was welcomed by Christians and also baptized.

Now at that time Pakistan and Afghanistan were embroiled in a border dispute. So it was not surprising that the Pakistanis thought Abraham was an Afghan spy and arrested him. After interrogating him, however, they finally released him and he immediately went into hiding.

When my wife and I visited Pakistan on vacation, we heard that Abraham had taken refuge in the home of a Danish missionary, so we went to see him there.

He was so happy to see us that he gave me the Afghan hug, which is three hugs—this side ... and that side ... and this side. Then we prayed together.

"They're after me in this country too," he told me. "What do you think I should do now?"

"What do you think God wants you to do?" I replied.

"I believe God wants me to go back to Afghanistan," he said. "If you will take my suitcases along with you when you return to Afghanistan, I will walk across the border again. Then I'll come to your home and pick up my things." So Abraham returned to Afghanistan on foot.

Now en route, a so-called guard robbed Abraham, took his turban and tied his wrists to his ankles. Then, with the butt of his gun, he pummeled him—just like the story the Lord told of the man who fell among thieves on the way from Jerusalem to Jericho.

As he called for help, local villagers came and rescued him. When Abraham finally reached Kabul, he found out that the judge who was going to try him was in prison himself, since he had opposed the authorities who had allowed women to remove the veil! Abraham returned to the government office where he had worked. They told him they had been looking all over for him, that he had received a promotion while he was away!

After that, Abraham returned to the States, to Oklahoma, where he received training to become a jet pilot for the Afghan Ariana Airlines. When he arrived in the States, he frequently gave his testimony of how he had come to receive Jesus Christ as his Lord and Savior.

Now several Muslims were also enrolled in that same training program. When they found out that Abraham had become a Christian, they sabotaged his plane.

Then while he was soloing, his plane crashed. He was killed instantly! We couldn't understand why God would allow one of the firstfruits for Christ in Afghanistan to die.

Abraham's body was flown back to Kabul and he was buried outside the city right next to the beautiful Paghman mountains, where he had lived.

My wife Betty and I went to see his family to express our sympathy. There we met his brother for the first time. The family took us to visit Abraham's grave.

Shortly afterwards, his brother came to see us.

He told us about a dream he had had. God often spoke to His people in dreams and visions throughout the Bible. Yet in our Western culture, if you say you had a dream, people immediately think you ate too much pizza.

"You know," the brother said, "I had a very strange dream the other night. I saw my dead brother Abraham. He was alive, standing in a beautiful garden where the trees were laden with the most luscious-looking fruit. A stream separated us, however. But the fruit looked so delicious I asked my brother to send me some."

(This is part of the Afghan custom of hospitality. Whenever you visit an orchard or vineyard when fruit is in season, the owners will give you a basketful.)

"When I asked my brother to do this," he went on, "Abraham replied, 'I'm sorry, I can't. But I'll tell you what to do. Go to the Wilsons' home and ask their son to tell you how to get to this garden. Then you can come here yourself and eat all the fruit you want.'" (Chris, our eldest boy, was nine years old then and a wonderful evangelist.)

"I've seen my dead brother alive in Heaven," Abraham's brother told me. "He sent me to your home. You must know the truth. What is it?"

Right there I shared the Gospel with him, telling him this was the way he could go to Heaven to be with his brother. And he accepted Christ right on the spot! Since then, he has gone on to become an even more wonderful Christian than his brother Abraham.

Shortly after that, Abraham's brother was also arrested for becoming a Christian, thrown into prison and given shock treatments to force him to deny his Lord. The authorities believed that he had truly lost his mind.

No sooner was he released from prison than Satan attacked his family. His little girl suddenly became gravely ill, and the local doctors gave her only a few days to live.

His wife had been keeping vigil at the child's bedside. One evening she was so exhausted that he told her to get some rest. "I'll take care of our little girl tonight," he said.

About 3:00 a.m., as he was reading his Pashtu New Testament, Abraham's brother suddenly beheld a radiant light flooding the entire room. Then he saw Jesus Christ appear in all His glory. The Lord spoke to him in perfect Pashtu without any accent.

"Don't be afraid," the Lord said. "Your little girl is going to be all right." Then the Lord disappeared.

When he turned to look at his little girl, she was healed!

He had never heard of anything like this before! So early the next morning he came to our home and told me all about it and asked for an explanation. Because he was such a young Christian, he had not yet read the Book of Acts where the Lord had appeared in a blinding vision to Saul on the road to Damascus. Neither had he read the book of Revelation to learn how the Lord appeared in a glorious vision to John on the island of Patmos.

I read those passages from the New Testament to him. When I had finished reading the description of Christ in Revelation, written by the Apostle John, this Afghan Christian turned to me and said: "That's exactly the way He looked! That's just the way He looked!"

"He has such a beautiful face. I can't wait to go and be with Him, the way my brother has."

Since that time, Abraham's brother has brought his whole family to Christ.

When we heard of the Russian invasion of Afghanistan, Betty and I were watching the news on television and saw the stream of refugees pouring across the border early in 1980. It broke our hearts to see that most of the refugees were children.

"How I'd love to go and help these people," I said to Betty. The Lord heard me. Within days we received a telephone call from World Concern, an evangelical relief agency, telling us they wanted to assist the Afghan refugees but wanted to find the best means of doing it. They asked if we would go and find a way for them to administer relief directly to the refugees.

Gordon-Conwell gave me permission to make the two-week trip, in the middle of the winter term. So we flew to Pakistan, on the border of Afghanistan, and helped reestablish a relief agency called SERVE (Serving Emergency Relief and Vocational Enterprises), which originally was started to help with a famine in Afghanistan in 1972 and which has continued ministering to the Afghan refugees. *(For more on this, please see "The Day Communism Began to Crumble," in Chapter 4.)*

When we arrived in Peshawar, Pakistan, whom should we meet on the street but this same Afghan Christian! The Russians had bombed his village, he told us, killing one of his children. But he had managed to escape and reach a safe haven in Pakistan with the rest of his family.

He was so thrilled to see us that not only did he give *me* the traditional Afghan triple hugs but he also gave one to Betty—something unheard of in his culture! But his joy exceeded all bounds.

A Muslim Priest Becomes A Beloved Physician

Dr. Saeed Khan was formerly a Kurdish Muslim priest whose job was to call the people to prayer from the minaret of his mosque. He wanted to study Christianity so he could win its followers to Islam. So when he had a chance to buy a stolen Bible in the bazaar, he quickly seized the opportunity. But it was while Saeed was reading the Bible that he came to faith in Jesus Christ.

When Saeed Khan read in the New Testament about communion and how Christ said to do this in remembrance of Him, he longed to take communion with His Lord. But there were no other Christians around. So he went out to a nearby vineyard, with a loaf of bread, picked some fresh grapes and squeezed them. Then, all alone, he ate the bread and drank the grape juice, just as Jesus had told His disciples to do. That was the only way he, a Muslim priest, could have communion with the Lord.

Here he was a Christian—yet he was still serving as the *muezzin* of a mosque, giving the call to prayer. At first he changed the words so that they sounded similar. But he wasn't satisfied with that.

Finally Saeed Khan could no longer keep silent about his new-found faith. He told his family that he had become a Christian. When his own brother Kaka tried to shoot him, Saeed fled from Kurdistan, in northwestern Iran.

He came to Hamadan, which is the old Ecbatana mentioned in Ezra 6:2 of the Bible and had once been the summer capital of the Persian empire. There he met some Christian missionaries who welcomed him into their home. But when the people of Hamadan heard that a Muslim priest had become a Christian and was with the missionaries, they began rioting and set out to lynch him.

The angry mob attacked the gates of the mission compound, trying to force their way in. But the gatekeeper had the presence of mind to ask them calmly:

"Why are you all excited about this man? He is not a Shi'ite Muslim but a Sunni. So what if a Sunni becomes a Christian. Why are you so excited about *that!*"

Well that hit home. These two divisions of Islam had been fighting each other for centuries. Almost immediately the Shi'ite leaders dismissed the mob, and the crowd dispersed.

Yet the missionaries knew that if Saeed stayed in Iran, he would be killed. So they sent him to study medicine in England and stay with Christians there. After he received his degree, he returned to Iran as a doctor. He even became the private physician to the Shah or King.

In time Dr. Saeed Khan became known as "The Beloved Physician of Tehran." His patients adored him. After treating his patients to the best of his ability, he would say to them: "Now I've done everything for you that my medical training has taught me. But there is still one thing more I can do for you."

"What's that?" they would ask him.

"I can pray for you. Would you give me permission to pray for you?" And with that, Dr. Saeed Khan would kneel down beside the patient's bed and ask the Lord to heal the person not only physically but spiritually as well.

Time after time, attempts were made on Dr. Saeed Kahn's life but in every instance God delivered him in a wonderful way. As the Psalmist writes in Psalm 34:7:

> *The angel of the Lord encamps round about those who fear Him and delivers them.*

Dr. Saeed Khan was not afraid of death. He knew God's protection.

Once when he was traveling to another city, he and his party decided to take a different route than they normally took. Later he learned that an ambush had been staked out on the original route, and he would have been killed had he traveled that road.

I remember hearing Dr. Saeed Khan give his testimony in the church in Tehran, when I was a young boy. My parents had sent me to Tehran for one year of schooling in the eighth grade before I came to the States. Inside, the church was packed. Outside, a heavily armed police guard surrounded the building to protect him against any assassins. The government of Iran respected Dr. Saeed Khan so highly that they did not want anyone to endanger the life of the man all Iran knew as "The Beloved Physician of Tehran."

His life story appears in the book *The Beloved Physician*, co-authored by Cady Allen and Jay Rasooli (Bromley, UK: STL, 1975).

"Father, Forgive Them ..."

Hassan Dehqani-Tafti was born in a little village in Iran called Taft.

Hassan left his village to attend the Christian school in Isfahan, the artistic center of the Muslim Shi'ite world. His father would cast lots each year to determine whether or not he should send Hassan to the Christian school, and every time the lot indicated that he should.

It was there that Hassan came to Christ.

I met Hassan at Cambridge University in England in the spring of 1948, when we were both students there.

At Cambridge, Hassan had run into higher criticism of the Bible for the first time, and it really concerned him. I remember the long hours we spent talking and praying together. He said that he knew the Bible was the Word of God because it was through the Bible that he had come to know the Living Christ Who had forgiven his sins and given him a new life. Yet now he was being taught all the things that were wrong with the Bible. He wondered if perhaps the Bible were like a beautiful stained glass window in a church which, although cracked, yet looks beautiful when the sunlight streams through it.

I tried to show Hassan that it wasn't the Bible that was cracked—it was the people who were teaching these doctrines!

Hassan and I had great times together there as students.

Then Hassan went back to Iran and became the Bishop for the Anglican Church there.

As a Christian leader in a Muslim country, Hassan had several attempts made on his life.

Shortly after the Ayatollah Khomeini took over Iran, several men broke into his bedroom early one morning and shot at him repeatedly as he lay in bed. His wife Margaret threw herself over him, and a bullet wounded her in the arm. Her blood soaked his pillow. However, he was untouched. The bullets ricocheted around his head but missed him completely.

The assassins then fled, thinking they had killed him.

After this, Hassan escaped from Iran and went to live in Cyprus.

He had an only son Bahram, who graduated from Oxford and was teaching English in Tehran. While Bahram was driving home one day, another car suddenly swerved in front of him and cut him off. Several men leaped out, dragged him from his car and threw him into their own. Then they drove outside the city limits where they shot and killed him.

Bishop Hassan Dehqani-Tafti couldn't return to Tehran for his son's funeral, since Khomeini was then in power. However, he sent a father's prayer for his son's murderers by telegram.

I would like to include it here. I believe it is one of the most powerful prayers I have heard in recent times. It reminds me of our Lord's intercession on the cross when he prayed: "Father, forgive them for they know not what they do." Hassan's prayer is written in the same spirit. It is called "A Father's Prayer for the Murderers of His Son."

> *Oh God, we remember not only Bahram but also his murderers, not because they killed him in the prime of his youth and made our hearts bleed and our tears flow, not because, with this savage act, they have brought further disgrace on the name of our country among civilized nations of the world, but because through their crime we now follow Thy footsteps more closely in the way of sacrifice.*
>
> *The terrible fire of this calamity burns up all selfishness and possessiveness in us. Its flame reveals the depth of depravity and meanness and suspicion, the dimension of hatred and the measure of sinfulness in human nature. It makes obvious, as never before, our need to trust God's love as shown in the cross of Jesus and His resurrection. Love which makes us free from hate towards our persecutors. Love which brings patience, forbearance, courage, loyalty, humility, generosity, greatness of heart. Love which more than ever deepens our trust in God's final victory and the eternal designs for the church and for the world. Love which teaches us how to prepare ourselves to face our own day of death.*
>
> *Oh God, Bahram's blood has multiplied the fruit of the Spirit in the soil of our souls. So when his murderers stand before Thee on the Day of Judgment, remember the fruit of the Spirit by which they have enriched our lives, and forgive.*

Hassan tells his story in the book, *Design of My World* (London, UK: USCL, 1962). He went to school in Isfahan, the capital of the empire. Isfahan was developed by one of the great Persian kings, Shah Abbas, a contemporary of Shakespeare in the early 1600's. Impressed with the Armenian Christians who lived to the north and were very accomplished in artistic crafts, the Shah transported an entire village of them down from their home in the the Caucasus and settled them outside his capital city of Isfahan, on the other side of the river, so that they could introduce their arts and crafts to his entire empire.

Ever since then, Isfahan has become the artistic capital of the Middle East. In fact, the Iranians have a saying "Isfahan Nisfi Jahan," which means "Isfahan is one half of the world."

There you find people painting pictures and delicate miniatures. In one bazaar, you will see them fashioning beautiful brass vases and trays.

In another, they are weaving exquisite rugs and carving designs in wood to stamp on decorated cloth.

The Shah Abbas hotel, which Khomeini destroyed, was one of the most beautiful in the world. Each room had an exquisite hand-painted mural. Everything was artistically designed.

Send Their Voice to the Ends of the Earth

An amazing invention—a record player made of flat cardboard—is taking the Gospel message where missionaries cannot go. It is designed to play Gospel messages in nearly 5,000 different languages!

All this came about because a lady missionary's health failed, preventing her return to the mission field.

Joy Ridderhof, an American, went to Honduras where she learned the language and preached the Gospel. However, after suffering a severe case of malaria, she was forced to return to the United States. Doctors would not allow her to go back to Honduras because she was too ill.

As Joy lay in bed, she cried out, "Lord, my heart is with the people in Central America. How can I serve You when I am so sick?"

And then she had an idea.

Although the doctors would not allow her to return to Honduras, she could still send her voice there. So she recorded her messages and sent them to her mission station.

At that time, the Yucatán peninsula in Mexico was off limits to missionaries. Some missionaries in Mexico knew a Christian man living there who was familiar with one of the languages of the Indians. The missionaries had an idea. "If we sent this man to the United States," they wrote to Joy Ridderhof, "would you work with him to record the Gospel message in the language of the Yucatán Indians? We will make sure the records reach them."

Of course, Joy was delighted and did just that. And through these messages, churches were established among this unreached peoples group.

From this small beginning, a magnificent idea was born: sending the Gospel on records where missionaries could not go. The idea took root and spread quickly.

Joy Ridderhof conceived the idea of recording Gospel messages for every language in the world. She started an organization called Gospel Recordings. They have now put the Gospel into 4,445 different languages!

When I was pastoring in Afghanistan, I received a letter from two women who worked with this organization. One was from Los Angeles, named Ann Sherwood, and the other was from France. Her name was Marlene Muir.

"If we come to Afghanistan," they wrote, "can we record the Gospel in any of the languages used by the Afghans?"

I wrote back, "I don't know. But pray and come, and we'll try."

So these two wonderful women came. They were real prayer warriors, and they prayed that they would be able to record Bible messages in every language in Afghanistan.

These women came well prepared. They brought state-of-the-art Swiss-made recording equipment that made no sound either when starting up or stopping. They converted one of the rooms in our home into a studio, covering the walls with styrofoam, and set up a special table with a microphone.

Now, at that time, Afghanistan had compulsory military service. Men drafted into the army came from every language group in the country. But finding a way to reach these men was a problem. If I had tried to enter the military camps, I would have been arrested as an American spy. However, we had an Afghan friend who had become a Christian. Being a national, he could easily mingle with the soldiers and get inside the military camps without causing suspicion.

Once inside the camps, he went around asking soldiers if they knew any men who spoke strange languages. When the soldiers would point out these men, our friend would go up to each one and speak to him in the main language which they had learned in the army. He would ask the soldier what part of the country he came from and what his language was.

Then he would arrange for these soldiers to visit our home on their one-day leave each week.

We would serve each one tea and cookies. Then I would speak to him in the main vernacular and would say:

"We want to make a recording of your language. Would you please tell us how you would say, in your tongue, 'Once there was a Good Shepherd.'"

The soldier would attempt this for us.

Then we would have him translate it back for us.

One soldier misunderstood and said: "Once there was a good sheep."

"No, no," I told him. "Not a sheep but someone who takes care of sheep."

"Oh," he said, "You would say it *this* way." And he corrected himself.

When we were sure he had the correct phrase, the two women would tape it. Then we would start on the next sentence. It took us more than three hours to record a three-minute message. But when we played it back, it sounded just like Billy Graham!

"How does this little machine know my language?" one soldier asked me. He had never heard his own voice nor seen a tape recorder before. Then he added, "You know, I never heard this before—that Jesus was our Good Shepherd, that He gave His life for us His sheep, that He came alive again on the third day and is alive now. And if we are sorry for our sins and ask Him to forgive us, He will cleanse us and give us everlasting life, because of His sacrifice. This is wonderful!"

Here he was preaching the Gospel to himself! Then he asked: "Why hasn't anyone told me this?"

The two women from Gospel Recordings were able to record Christian messages in all fifty-one languages spoken in Afghanistan.

Although Gospel Recordings has produced these recordings, you won't find electricity in many outlying places to run a tape recorder. So some Christian engineers came up with a brilliant idea. It's a manual record player made of cardboard, and has a needle which you put right on the edge. Then with a stick or pencil, you turn it by hand. You can easily play this anywhere in the world. Many who have heard the Gospel this way have come to Christ.

The Language of the Heart

Before I went to Afghanistan in 1951, I sought the advice of Dr. Samuel Zwemer, who was probably the greatest missionary to Muslims in history.

"Dr. Zwemer," I asked, "if you were going to Afghanistan now, what would be the single most important thing you would do?"

"I would learn the proverbs of the people," he replied. "Because it is through their proverbs that you touch their hearts. Proverbs will give you the illustrations you need for your messages, sermons, and daily conversation."

I found this to be very true. When you learn the proverbs of a people in Asia, you touch them in a way that nothing else can.

My wife Betty and I were invited to dinner at the home of Christians, Jim and Margaret Cudney, who worked at the American Embassy. The dinner guests included some Afghan officials in Kabul. After being invited in to the delicious meal prepared by our hostess, one Afghan official said to me, "What, no cocktails?"

18 "More To Be Desired Than Gold"

In response, I quoted an Afghan proverb to him: "If you only have bread and onions, still you should have a happy face."

His face grew red. He confessed, "Oh, I said a terrible thing to you."

After that, whenever I met him, he would say, "You're a much better Muslim than I am." (Muslims are not supposed to drink alcohol.)

I had no idea what a powerful effect this proverb would have on him.

When I was in Afghanistan, I collected some of these sayings and produced a small book called *One Hundred Afghan Proverbs*. The Afghans loved it. I have had to reprint it here in the States because so many Afghan refugees have continued to ask me for it.

Many of these refugees have visited our home and have read this book. Although they knew these proverbs very well, they would laugh and laugh over them. They would slap their knees as they laughed—you would think they were hearing them for the very first time. The Afghans have liked my book of proverbs so much that two of them have reprinted it verbatim, but under their own names!

The late Dr. Donald A. McGavran, former missionary to India and founder of Fuller Theological Seminary's School of World Mission, in Pasadena, California, said that language accounts for more than 60 percent of the culture—that's why it's so important to learn the language of a people. Language not only helps you communicate but it also helps you understand the people and appreciate their culture.

The Orientals love proverbs. If you can quote an appropriate one, it can have the force of Scripture. Unfortunately, most Westerners look on proverbs as passé and many don't even enjoy reading the book of Proverbs. Yet Billy Graham reads one chapter from the Book of Proverbs each day. He values it that much.

A Medical Student Meets the Great Physician

When I was a student, I met a young Muslim from Turkey who had come to the United States to study medicine. While he was working in a hospital, he contracted tuberculosis and was forced to spend several months in bed. There in his hospital room, while he was recuperating, Farouk Konuk listened intently while I shared the Gospel with him and gave him a New Testament.

I told Farouk that I loved the country of Turkey because it played such an important part in the Bible.

"It does?" he said. "What do you mean?"

"The man who wrote the greatest number of books in the New Testament, the Apostle Paul, was also from Turkey. He came from

Tarsus, along the southern shore of Turkey." Immediately Farouk became interested. He had never heard anything like this before.

"While the Apostle Paul was traveling through Turkey," I continued, "a man joined him. His name was Dr. Luke. He too came from Turkey and wrote both the Acts and the Gospel of Luke."

Furthermore, I told him, while John the Apostle was in Ephesus, he was captured by the Romans and exiled to the Island of Patmos as a prisoner.

I remember that one of the most thrilling trips I ever took was to the Island of Patmos with Dr. Bob Pierce, who founded World Vision. The only way you can get there is by ship.

We sailed through the Greek islands and came to the Island of Patmos, a beautiful little gem in the blue Aegean Sea in the Mediterranean. There we visited the grotto where John is believed to have had the vision he describes in the book of Revelation. It's very interesting that this cave faces Turkey, and from its entrance you can see the mountains of Asia Minor.

If you read Revelation and Christ's message to the seven churches, our Lord mentions these seven cities in a sequence that forms an exact circle facing Patmos. Christ starts with Ephesus, which was nearest, and goes all the way around to Laodicea in the east. The chances of that happening by coincidence, I calculated, would be one in more than 5,040! Isn't the Bible wonderful the way its facts can be confirmed!

I told Farouk that the Apostle John—who also wrote the Gospel of John and the Letters of John—had also lived in Turkey. Together with Paul's and Luke's writings, right there you have most of the New Testament writings coming straight from Turkey!

Well, Farouk was so thrilled to hear all this that he read the New Testament straight through. When he had finished, I asked him if he would like to accept Jesus Christ as his personal Savior.

"Oh yes!" he answered. He had come to realize that this was all part of his background. The spirit of nationalism, the love for his country had so stirred his heart that he had read the Bible for himself. Now, for the first time, he saw Christianity in a different light, antedating Islam. It took him back to his real roots. And so he was ready to accept the Lord.

In sharing the Gospel with Muslims, it's so important to find redemptive analogies. It's especially helpful to associate Christianity with their homeland.

For example, when Billy Graham went to Africa, he said he was so glad to be on the continent where his Lord Jesus Christ took his first steps, because Christ probably learned to walk on the continent of Africa.

If you go to Egypt, you can share that with the people. They probably have never heard that Jesus learned to walk there. That makes them feel they have a real part in the history of Christianity. You can tell them how Jesus' parents had to flee to Egypt to escape from Herod, who tried to kill the Child, that Jesus grew up as a refugee boy in Egypt, and that His family stayed in Egypt until the cruel king died.

Another example of redemptive analogies is the Nestorian cross featured in the patterns of Afghan rugs. When we first went to Afghanistan, there were no Christians there. Yet, we saw these beautiful Nestorian crosses woven in their carpet designs, designs which they have been weaving for centuries. The patterns have been handed down from father to son, from mother to daughter.

However, when you go to their homes and see these crosses, and ask them if they know what the crosses symbolize, they will reply, "No. We have no idea." Then you can tell them the story of the cross and the way Jesus died on it as a sacrifice for their sins.

"Your ancestors knew why. This is what they believed and this is why they put this design into the carpets."

Only A Scrap of Paper

Before he became a Methodist Bishop in India, Subhan had been a Sufi Muslim preparing for the priesthood. In school, it was common to hear his instructors attack Christianity.

But one day while Subhan was walking home from class, he noticed a scrap of paper tossed by the wind across his path. It turned out to be a page from Matthew's Gospel, describing the crucifixion and death of Christ.

"My God, My God, why has Thou forsaken Me?" He read the words over and over again.

Now this astonished Subhan. He had been taught that Jesus Christ had not really been crucified but that Christ's likeness had fallen on Judas. It was Judas who had hung on that cross, not Jesus. Christ had ascended to Heaven before the crucifixion.

Subhan read and reread that single sentence again and again. "These are not the words of Judas," he thought to himself. "Judas would have known why God had forsaken him. These are *not* the words of an evil man. They are the words of a good man. Only a good man could have asked, 'My God, My God, why hast Thou forsaken Me?'"

Suddenly he *knew* that it was really Christ who had died on that cross, not Judas. And he accepted Christ as his Savior.

Subhan then shared this revelation with his fellow students at the Muslim school. One day in class, while the professor was in the midst of a particularly bitter attack against Christianity, one of the students raised his hand.

"We have a Christian in our class," he announced.

"Who is that?" demanded the professor. The student pointed to Subhan.

"Subhan is a Christian," said the student.

"Subhan, are you a Christian?" asked the professor.

"I believe Jesus died on the cross for my sins," replied Subhan.

The professor became furious! He hastily dismissed the class and rushed to the principal's office. They decided to hold a faculty meeting and order Subhan to appear before them.

Although he was a very young Christian, the Holy Spirit gave Subhan a wisdom beyond human understanding. He was amazed at the answers that came out of his mouth at that faculty meeting.

Finally the faculty proclaimed him guilty of heresy and expelled him before the whole school.

But he told me his heart was filled with unspeakable joy at the privilege of suffering for his Lord.

After that, Subhan began studying for the Christian ministry. The first seminary turned out to be liberal one in India. He realized they didn't have the truth as he knew it from the Scriptures. He next tried a Roman Catholic seminary. But while they didn't attack the Bible, they ignored it altogether. So he left and finally entered an evangelical seminary which emphasized the Scriptures. Later he became a Methodist Bishop in India.

The Itinerant Preacher Who Pulled Teeth

Mansur Sang was a very devout Muslim Sufi who became a Baha'i. From his home in Iran, he had even made a pilgrimage to the sacred Baha'i shrine in Acre in Haifa, Israel. Yet he became disillusioned with that religion. Then he heard the Gospel and accepted Christ as his Savior.

In the Muslim religion, Mansur had been a dervish, a group of Sufis who perform various feats to earn their salvation. Some of them whirl around until they just fall into a stupor. Others simply torture themselves. They will eat nails and even break light bulbs to chew and swallow the jagged pieces. Sometimes they will take a sword and plunge it through their cheeks and into their mouth, or pierce their flesh with sharp instruments, torturing themselves in order to reach a higher level of ecstasy and so earn their salvation.

Some dervishes will give away everything they own and wander as mendicants, with bowls hung around their necks, begging for food from house to house.

Mansur Sang had been that kind of dervish.

After he accepted Christ, however, he decided he wanted to become a *Christian* dervish. No longer would he live by begging. Now he would have a profession—even as the the Apostle Paul once had. And so he became a dentist. That's how I came to know him when I was a boy in Iran.

One of the medical missionaries, a doctor, gave Mansur a pair of forceps. He carried these forceps on him as he walked from village to village, asking people if anyone had a toothache and wanted a tooth pulled. Now, in Afghanistan, I've seen barbers often serve as dentists. They would pull out a pair of forceps, grasp the patient's tooth—then with one foot firmly anchored against the patient's shoulder, they would both push and pull at the same time. This works wonderfully every single time!

Well, Mansur would pull people's teeth in the village square, always attracting a crowd. By the time he had extracted the tooth, the crowd had grown substantially.

This was the moment Mansur had been waiting for. Opening his Bible, he would start preaching the Gospel. Now Mansur couldn't read or write a single word but he had memorized much of the Bible. He only used the open Bible so people would know the source of the passages he quoted.

Once Mansur Sang was arrested by the police for preaching on the streets in Shiraz in southern Iran. When they brought him to the prison, the jailer said, "Why have you arrested this man again? He is happier in prison than he is outside. And besides, he makes Christians out of the other prisoners. I don't want him here." But they put him in prison, nevertheless.

The chief of police was a Baha'i. When he heard that this Muslim convert to Christianity was in jail, he ordered him brought to his office. They had confiscated the bag of Scripture portions Mansur Sang took with him everywhere.

The police chief pulled out one leaflet and asked him what it was. Mansur Sang answered that it was Christ's Sermon on the Mount. He asked what it cost. Mansur Sang said that he gave it away free to anyone who agreed to read it or have it read to him.

The chief of police laughed. "This shows your religion isn't worth anything. You have to give your literature away."

He then pointed to a shelf of Baha'i books and said, "I paid hundreds of *tomans* for these. This shows how much more valuable my religion is than yours."

The Lord Jesus Christ said that when we are persecuted for His sake, the Holy Spirit would give us the ability to answer effectively. Mansur Sang pointed to the electric light that was burning in the office and asked, "Do you pay money for this?"

The chief of police said, "Yes, we are happy to pay for electricity and these fixtures."

Then Mansur Sang pointed to the sun that was shining outside. He asked, "Do you pay money for the sunshine?"

The chief answered, "No."

Then Mansur Sang said, "Your books—like these electric light fixtures—are man-made and give a little light, but you have to pay for them. This Scripture is the Word of God and has the light of the sun. And just the way sunshine is free, so this is free to those who will receive it."

The God Who Heals

Muslims respond to signs and wonders, especially miracles of healing. When my wife and I were in Afghanistan, the sick would regularly come knocking at our door, asking me to pray for them.

At first I would tell them I was not a medical doctor. But the Afghans would reply, "We know you're not a medical doctor but we know you pray. We want you to pray for us so God will heal us."

So I would pray for them, and God healed many. This is a wonderful way to reach Muslims.

As Christians, we need to be more sensitive to the physical needs of Muslims. They yearn to see a God who acts in power today.

T. L. Osborne and his wife served as missionaries to the Muslims in India for fifteen years. During that time, they saw very few Muslims come to Christ.

Then during one of their furloughs home to the States, the Osbornes attended a healing service where they saw miracles happen and people receive Christ. As soon as they returned to India, they began to pray for the sick each time they preached the Gospel. And God healed many Muslims.

When Muslims saw people being healed before their very eyes, more of them came to Christ in a single night than they had in the previous fifteen years the Osbornes had served in India! Muslims saw the power of the Living Christ and they wanted to know Him.

Unfortunately, as Christians, we have neglected the ministry of healing. Yet Jesus healed. Paul healed. The apostles healed. In fact, Jesus said, "The works that I do, you will do also, and you will do greater works than these because I go to My Father."

There is nothing greater than a demonstration of the Spirit's power to convince Muslims of Christ's power. Muslims love to argue. Yet when they see the power of God made manifest and the sick healed in the Name of Jesus, they come to Christ more readily.

He Slipped In the Back Door

The young man was obviously a stranger, standing there on a main street in Kabul, Afghanistan. With his flowing red beard, big black hat and black suit, he certainly cut an imposing figure. At first I thought he was a rabbi.

When I asked him if he spoke English, he replied, "Yes, I do."

"May I help you? I know the local language," I offered.

"Yes, I am looking for someone by the name of Christy Wilson."

I couldn't figure out who he was and why he was looking for me!

He turned out to be a Mennonite from Ohio. On closer look, I noticed that his black suit had no buttons, just hooks and eyes. So I asked him what he was doing there in Afghanistan.

"My wife and I are in the state of Swat," he said. Swat was a Muslim state in northern Pakistan that was completely closed to Christian missions. I asked him what he was doing there.

"I'm teaching English in a secondary school," he said. "And my wife and I are having a great time. We invite students to our home and teach them English using the New Testament as a textbook."

Since I knew no missionaries were allowed in that Muslim state, I asked, "How did you ever get into Swat?"

"I had never heard of the place before," he told me. "I applied under a Fulbright Scholarship to teach English in Germany, and they sent me to Swat." Now he and his wife were tentmakers teaching English in a closed Muslim country!

Tentmaking has a Biblical basis. The Apostle Paul himself was a tentmaker who supported himself while carrying on his ministry (Acts 18). Muslims themselves have been tentmakers and so they understand when others take secular jobs to witness among them.

This couple's experience reminds me of a wonderful truth once expressed by that great woman of God, Mildred Cable, of England. She worked in the Gobi Desert of China among the Muslims.

"No country is closed to God," she said. "If the front door is closed, try the back door." Tentmaking is going in the back door.

As someone once pointed out, "It's only real friends who are allowed to come in the back door. The others have to go in the front door." If the front door has a sign "No Missionaries Allowed," then go in the back door as a tentmaker.

Waldron Scott, the former secretary of World Evangelical Fellowship, believes tentmaking will be the next great Christian movement—growing even larger than today's missions movement.

Nationalism vs. Islam: The Thread That Unravels?

Nothing has done more to undermine the unity of the Muslim world than nationalism. In a sense, nationalism has become a religion in many Islamic countries, a religion of national secularism. And it often wields a far stronger power than Islam.

For example, the Sunnis once had an elected Caliph who ruled the entire Muslim world, very much like the Pope in Roman Catholicism. Yet since 1924, when the last Caliph died in Turkey, the Sunnis have not been able to choose a successor because Muslims now vote exclusively along national lines. The King of Saudi Arabia would like to become the Caliph, but other Islamic nations will not accept him.

Often Islamic groups try to dictate policies in a country, but the national government puts them down.

Indeed, nationalism has broken up the Muslim world.

A case in point is Afghanistan in 1959, when the government decided to allow women to remove their veil—despite Islamic opposition. A direct confrontation with Islam followed—but nationalism emerged victorious.

It all started when a writer from the States, Ed Hunter, came to Kabul, Afghanistan to "introduce Afghanistan to the rest of the world," as he put it.

Ed had been a correspondent in the Far East for about 30 years. He coined the term "brainwashing" after observing the way the Communists indoctrinated people through psychological techniques. He wrote several books on the subject, one entitled *Brainwashing in Red China* (New York: Vanguard Press, 1951). He also wrote another called *Brainwashing: The Story of Men Who Defied It* (New York: Farrar, 1956). The ones who withstood brainwashing, he discovered, had a strong faith in Jesus Christ.

One day Ed told me, "You know, I haven't been to a church service since I was a little boy in Sunday School. But I've been so impressed with the way that Christians have withstood brainwashing that I've decided there really must be something to Christianity after all."

Ed lived in Afghanistan for an entire year, attending church regularly. During that year, he researched and wrote a book that precipitated the bloody clash between nationalism and Islam. It was entitled *The Past Present* (London: Hoddard & Stoughton, 1959). The premise of his book was this: if you want to go to the one place in the world where you will see the past in the present, go to Afghanistan. And the book jacket featured a photo showing four women wearing veils.

In his research, Ed interviewed more than 1,000 people for his book. One was an Afghan woman behind a veil. He even met with the Prime Minister and the King himself.

While Ed was still gathering material, I asked him, "What do you hope to accomplish through your book?"

"Well," he replied, "when my book comes out, the veil will be torn off."

I thought that was a wild claim, to say the least. Muslim women had been wearing the veil for centuries, since Mohammed's time. Yet, amazingly enough, that's exactly what happened. Shortly after the book was published in Great Britain in the spring of 1959, the Afghan government ordered women to remove the veil.

The book was a bombshell. It opened with the author's statement that upon arriving in Afghanistan, he found the date on the Muslim calendar to be in the 1300's. And as far as progress was concerned, the culture did date back to the 1300's, according to the Western calendar. From there, he set out to "introduce Afghanistan to the rest of the world."

Ed spared nothing in his analysis. He wrote glowingly about the marvelous work being done by the American engineering and construction companies in Afghanistan who were building dams, airports, canals, and highways. By way of contrast, he compared the efficiency of those in private enterprise with those working in the U.S. government bureaucracy.

When employees of the Morrison-Knutsen Company heard that Ed Hunter had many kind words to say about them, they couldn't wait to read it. Regular mail would take too long from England, so they had it shipped by air. Can you imagine forty-six copies of this book arriving at the airport—waiting for a customs official to inspect the package!

(If the package had been sent by regular mail, they could have picked it up in Pakistan, brought it in by car, and there would have been no trouble at all.)

When one of the American construction workers went to the airport to pick up the books, the customs official opened the package and gasped when he saw those forty-six books, all featuring the photo of four Afghan women in veils.

"This is a terrible book!" the customs official exclaimed. "Why are you importing this book into Afghanistan?"

"We didn't know what the book was about when we ordered it," replied the American.

"You're lying," said the officer. "No one would order forty-six copies of a book unless he knew exactly what it was all about."

So the customs official confiscated the whole lot. He then distributed copies of the book to all the key national leaders, including the King, the Prime Minister, and cabinet members, to show them the terrible things that had been written about Afghanistan. When the King read the book, he quickly met with his advisors to decide what to do.

"We knew that one day we would have to allow women to remove their veils," they said. "But now that the rest of the world is ridiculing us, we must do it right away."

The summer of 1959, shortly after the book was published, Afghanistan held its annual national celebration. Only this year, all Afghan officials were ordered to attend the official ceremonies with their wives. And their wives were required to appear without their veils!

My wife and I attended these official ceremonies, and it was interesting to see how the Afghan wives dressed for this gala event. They all wore dark glasses with kerchiefs covering their heads. Their ankle-length coats with long sleeves almost gave the appearance of a flowing veil. Nevertheless, this new dress code really sent shock waves throughout Afghan society.

The Muslims reacted violently to this development. Since the judicial system was in the hands of the Muslim priests, the *mullahs* who served as judges incited riots against the Afghan Government. The Government arrested the reactionary judges and threw them into prison.

The riots also extended as far away as Kandahar, in southern Afghanistan. first they attacked everything that was modern. They overturned cars and set them on fire. They destroyed the movie theater, gutting it completely. They ransacked the schools, especially the schools for girls, where they killed some of the teachers.

Then they directed their fury against the homes of foreigners.

The first American home they came to, the lady's husband was away working at the new airport. Although she was home all alone at the time, she was a very resourceful woman, having served as a police officer back in Seattle, Washington. She knew just how to handle a riot.

As the hostile mob stormed into her front garden, she waited until they reached her front door and tried to break it down. Then she cocked her high-powered rifle, aimed it carefully at the glass transom over the door, and fired a volley of shots. Shattered glass showered the rioters. To a man, they retreated from her garden—like a wave rolling back.

Then the Afghan government called out the army and, using Russian tanks, the soldiers fired the cannons into the rioting crowds and killed hundreds of people.

Shortly after that, Bob Pierce, Paul Rees, and Larry Ward of World Vision came to Afghanistan and asked me to go with them to visit a hospital in Isfahan, Iran. World Vision wanted to help the hospital, which had no modern plumbing but relied on hand pumps.

We left Kabul and arrived at Kandahar, the scene of violent rioting, on the first leg of our flight. As we prepared for take-off again, the door on the airplane, a DC 4, would not close. First the flight attendant tried to shut the door and failed. Then he called on the flight engineer, the co-pilot and the pilot to help him. None of them could close the door. We were told that if our plane did not take off before 4:00 p.m., we would not be able to make the trip that day. Afghanistan had no night landing facilities. Moreover, we needed time to return to the Kandahar airport to land before nightfall, if anything should go wrong in flight. But the door just would not stay closed.

Four o'clock came, and the door still was not working, so our flight was postponed until the next day. Although the government had closed Kandahar to outsiders because of the riots, we had nowhere else to spend the night. So they had no choice but to take us into the city despite the unrest there.

I took Dr. Paul Rees around to the homes of Americans and we called on people who had gone through the riots.

One USAID official had hurried from house to house, warning people of the rioting mobs and urging them to stay indoors, and not to go out on the streets. The rioters seized this man and tried to kill him, stabbing him over and over again—right in front of the home of an American nurse. Immediately the servants of this nurse rushed out, grabbed the man, and pulled him into the house to safety. There the nurse immediately treated his multiple stab wounds, saving his life.

I'll never forget the scene when Dr. Paul Rees and I went to visit this man. He had fresh stab wounds all over his body and lay weak from the loss of blood. Sitting beside the man, Dr. Rees opened his Bible and read to him from Psalm 103:

> *Bless the Lord, O my soul;*
> *And all that is within me, bless His Holy name!*
> *Bless the Lord, O my soul,*
> *And forget not all His benefits;*
> *Who forgives all your iniquities;*
> *Who heals all your diseases;*
> *Who redeems your life from destruction.*

I looked at the wounded man's eyes. Tears were streaming down his face. Dr. Rees read, talked and prayed with him in his compassionate pastoral bedside manner. It was providential that we had been forced to stop in Kandahar that night.

The next morning, we boarded the plane. This time the door closed easily. However, as we approached the end of the runway, we heard a loud explosion! A tire had blown out. The whole plane tilted to one side. We all roared with laughter.

But World Vision vice-president Larry Ward, who had been a jet pilot during World War II, quickly dispelled our mirth. "Don't laugh. This is serious," he said. "If it had happened during take-off or landing, we would all have been killed."

That afternoon, after the tire had been changed, we finally left Kandahar for Iran.

The Moon Rock

When I was teaching in Afghanistan in the 1950's, there was a Muslim priest in the same school who taught the students that the world was flat. The students were confused. If this were so, they reasoned, then how could their American teachers leave Afghanistan, travel west, go around the world and return from the east?

"If you don't believe the world is flat," the Muslim priest said, "then you're heretics and deserve to be killed."

According to this same Muslim priest, since the world is flat, the sun circles the earth and goes through the fires of hell each night. That's what heats up the sun—the fires of hell. Then the sun comes out and warms the world. But in autumn, Satan becomes lazy and does not stoke the fires, causing the flames to cool down—which is why the sun's rays are cooler in winter. Then when Satan begins stoking the flames again, we get the heat of summertime.

While Russia and America were competing to land the first man on the moon in the 1960's, some Muslim theologians argued: "No living person can go to the moon because it's in heaven. And you can't go to heaven until you die," they reasoned.

"Moreover," they added, "since the moon is the Muslims' holy symbol, God would never allow a Russian atheist or an American heretic to get there first. It would have to be a Muslim, if anyone!"

After America's Neil Armstrong landed on the Moon, many in the Islamic world claimed he became a Muslim the moment he set foot on the moon!

Then the United States Government sent a small lunar rock sample to Afghanistan for the people to view. They were thinking only in terms of advanced technology. They did not grasp its implications for Muslim theology.

Many Afghans eagerly stood in line for hours to view the moon rock. I stood in line with them. Finally I saw it! The lunar rock was set on prongs, encased in a clear plastic bubble, rotating slowly under bright spotlights. It was very impressive.

Standing in front of me was a Muslim priest, over 6 feet tall, wearing a large white turban. He kept everyone waiting while he scrutinized the moon rock from all angles. Finally, he shouted in a booming voice: "It's all a big lie! I've seen rocks around here that look just like this! This is no moon rock. It's just a plain old stone!"

Seeing Is Believing

A friend of mine was riding on a bus in Pakistan when two Muslims, seated in front of him, began arguing. One said that Jesus didn't die on the cross, which is the traditional Islamic view. The other contended that He did.

"How do you know He died on the cross?"

"I saw it in the movie *Ben Hur*," the other replied.

It's amazing how even secular movies on the life of Christ have a dramatic impact on Muslims.

When I was a little boy in Iran, a very popular movie, *King of Kings*, depicted the life of Christ. It was only a silent movie but how the Muslims flocked to see this drama! If secular movies have such power to move Muslims, imagine the impact that top-notch Christian movies and videos could have on them.

"My Sins Are Forgiven"

Hajji Sultan Mohammed and his family were driven out of Afghanistan in the late 1800's because of politics, and went to live in India. He went on a pilgrimage to Mecca and became an Islamic scholar. In India he joined a group of Muslims who were trying to win others to their faith.

One day, Sultan met a Hindu who had come to Christ. He heard this man say that he had become a Christian, "Because in Christ I found all my sins are forgiven."

This went straight to Sultan's heart. He studied the Koran and other Muslim holy books, as well as writings on Hinduism, Buddhism and other religions, to see if they too promised the same forgiveness of sins.

Not one of them did. Only Christ offered this.

"My sins are forgiven." These words kept tugging at his heart. Sultan accepted Jesus as his Savior. You can read his testimony in the booklet, *Why I Became A Christian*, published by the Gospel Literature Service in Bombay, India.

The Legacy

Pastor Christoffel, from Germany, was a missionary who pioneered in schools for the blind. He first started one in Turkey and then another in Iran, where he worked with my parents in Tabriz, in the province of Azerbaijan.

My father had the blind students take turns leading the church services by reading with their fingers from their Braille Bibles.

During World War II, Pastor Christoffel was interned as an enemy alien, but he served as a chaplain there in the camp. Following the War, he ran two schools in Isfahan, Iran, one for boys and another for girls. He also had a vision to extend this ministry by starting a work in the future with the blind in Afghanistan.

After his death, the two schools in Isfahan were renamed the Christoffel Mission to the Blind. The Mission generously supported our work with the blind in Afghanistan because of Pastor Christoffel's vision. When we began teaching the blind in Kabul, the Mission's leader, Pastor Sigfried Wiesinger, came to Afghanistan and not only gave us advice but funds as well. He also supplied us with personnel, equipment, and a library of Braille books in German.

Today the Christoffel Mission to the Blind has work in 65 countries, and an annual income of more than $15 million.

It's thrilling to see what God does through one person who counts all but loss for the excellency of the knowledge of Christ and sought to show His love to the handicapped. Pastor Christoffel did this.

Never Underestimate the Power of a Woman

The Muslims have often treated women as second-class citizens and, in certain places, do not permit them to drive cars.

My daughter, Nancy Newbrander, lived in Saudi Arabia for two years while her husband was a hospital administrator there. They were in Tobuk, in the northwest part, near Jordan, serving as tentmakers.

For those two years, my daughter was not allowed to drive.

Then the Gulf War started and Saudi Arabia invited the United States to help them.

As the U.S. Army troops rolled through one day, a Saudi traffic officer stopped one army vehicle. The driver was a woman soldier.

"Get out," he ordered. "No women are allowed to drive here."

The woman reached over to the seat next to her, picked up her high-powered automatic rifle and aimed it directly at him.

"It's okay, you can go through," the officer stammered.

The Hidden Meaning of Numbers

The Baha'is, a cult of Islam, want to change the calendar to show nineteen months, each with nineteen days, plus four days of celebration. This is based on the numerical value of one of the names of God—*wahid* (or "19"). *Wahid* means "one." God is *Wahid*, or God is one.

In the Middle East, it is very common to know the numerical values of the letters of the alphabet. That's why in Revelation we are told that the number of the Antichrist will add up to 666.

I came to discover the numerical value of letters in an embarrassing way. When I taught English in Afghanistan, I had to take attendance at every class. So I would number the students and give them places accordingly. Once, when I reached number 39, the class just exploded. They began to laugh and clap and jump up and down and whistle! I lost complete control of them. I couldn't imagine what had happened. Finally it all died down, and we went on with our lesson.

After class, I asked a student what the commotion was all about. "The number 39 which you assigned to that student," he said, "is the numerical value of two very bad swear words. It was just as if you had called him profane names."

Which all goes to show you how very important it is to understand the culture of the people with whom you serve.

A Muslim Army Officer Comes to Christ

When the Ayatollah Khomeini ordered women to return to the old tradition of wearing the veil in public, as they had in Mohammed's time, many women openly rebelled in Tehran. There were riots and demonstrations. Many threatened to become Christians rather than comply.

As a result, Muslims flocked to Christian churches in Iran. From the very beginning of Khomeini's takeover, in fact, Iranians have purchased more Bibles than ever before in the history of their country. The Bible Society could not keep up with the demand and ran out of Scriptures! Rush orders were sent to Taiwan for printing more Persian Bibles.

During this period a very interesting thing happened here.

A former colonel in the Shah's army had barely escaped death at Khomeini's hands before he finally found refuge in Danvers, Massachusetts. He had left Iran with very little. He did not even have a pension anymore, because of the Ayatollah. So the Colonel sent his wife back to Tehran to sell their property and take care of their business matters.

Now, although women were required to wear a veil, they were still free to travel in and out of the country without any of the restrictions that applied to men. So the Colonel's wife prepared to return to Tehran.

"When you go back," her husband told her, "I want you to buy me a Persian Bible."

Being a very zealous Muslim, she certainly didn't want to buy a Bible. Yet since her husband had told her to, she had to obey him. So she bought a Bible in Tehran and brought it back with her.

Now the Colonel's wife was a very superstitious woman. She didn't even like the idea of being in the same room with the Bible. She was afraid it would cast a spell over her.

Yet as she watched her husband read the Bible with great enjoyment, she became more and more curious. finally she decided to see for herself what was so compelling about this Book. Every morning when he would leave for work, she would slip into the room, secretly open the Bible, and begin reading it.

Well, she accepted Jesus Christ as her Lord before *he* did. Later he came to Christ himself.

Their only son was accepted at a university in Florida. Since the parents wanted to be near him, the father went to Florida to search for a home to rent. But he found only homes that were for sale.

One day while the Colonel was in Florida house-hunting, his wife was on her knees praying that the Lord would guide her husband. Unknown to her, even while she was praying, her husband came across an outdoor tent meeting revival. So he walked in. He wanted to ask if anyone knew of a house for rent but hesitated. Dressed as he was in his army fatigues, he didn't think he looked presentable. So he decided against it.

After the tent meeting was over, he went to a nearby Burger King to get some supper. As he walked into the restaurant, whom should he meet but the very pastor who had been leading the revival meeting. He was there with his teenage children.

"Didn't I see you at the back of the tent?" asked the pastor.

"Yes," the Colonel replied.

So the pastor started a conversation with him, asking him where he was from and what he was doing in Florida.

"Well, I'm looking for a house to rent."

"You know," said the pastor, "a member of my congregation sells real estate, and only today he told me that he has a house for rent and doesn't know what to do with it—since he only sells houses. Here is his name and phone number. Why don't you call him?"

The Colonel phoned the real estate agent, and the man was happy to rent him the house.

So the Colonel and his wife are down in Florida. Recently I talked to them and asked them if they had found a church. "Oh yes," they said, "We found a very good 'baptized church.'"

When You Put Your Hand to the Plow ...

One afternoon several years ago, I was driving through the Afghan countryside with some American friends. We weren't in any particular hurry, so we stopped the car when we saw an Afghan farmer plowing his field with a team of oxen.

Few scenes portray so well the life of an Afghan peasant, so we each took several pictures. Little did we realize what was going through the farmer's mind. He apparently had never seen a camera before, and for all he knew, the long lenses could have been gun barrels or cannons pointing in his direction. Several times he glanced over his shoulder at us with a concerned look on his face.

Then I noticed something else. Before we had arrived on the scene, all of his plowed furrows were straight. He had set his sights on a landmark in the distance, and had guided his team of oxen in a direct line to that point. However, when he looked back at us, the furrow began to weave back and forth.

For the first time, I understood the meaning of Christ's parable about the plow. Jesus said, "No one, after putting his hand to the plow and looking back is fit for the Kingdom of God" (Luke 9:62).

If we are to plow straight furrows, we must keep looking ahead to Jesus, the Author and Finisher of our faith.

In most of the stories of this chapter, we have taken a look at the furrows God has been plowing in Afghanistan—one of the world's most "closed" countries to the Gospel. But it was written with Afghanistan's future in mind.

Hosea 10:12 says, "Break up your fallow ground for it is time to seek the Lord until He comes to rain righteousness on you."

It is also my prayer that others will be challenged to pray for the people of Afghanistan and the other lost sheep in the Muslim world. It is my prayer that still others will seek God's will about possibly serving in Afghanistan, or working with Afghan refugees, or ministering in another country deeply influenced by the pillars of Islam, or witnessing to Muslim students studying around the world.

Yes, religious liberty is often curtailed in Islamic lands, and if you were to measure missionary success by the number of Christian converts, countries like Afghanistan, Iran, Saudi Arabia, and Libya would be at the bottom of the list. Some mission experts have gone so far as to label these lands a "green harvest" and have raised objections to sending witnesses into resistant Muslim areas. They argue that it is much wiser to expand efforts among receptive peoples where the results in converts are greater.

However, I strongly disagree. Even a green harvest needs care and preparation for the time when it ripens. Outstanding men and women of God have labored in Muslim lands, and others are needed to enter into their labors.

Dr. William Miller, who spent forty-three years as a missionary in Iran has said, "The main reason there have been so few Muslims who have come to Christ is not due so much to the perversity of the fish, as it is to the paucity of the fishers."

Our Lord has told us to preach the Gospel to every creature, and this includes Muslims. In the battle for people's souls, Satan's strongholds need to be attacked. The Great Commission is the God-given sequel to Christ's incarnation, crucifixion and resurrection. It is not a man-made directive, but a divine imperative.

Jesus came that we might go, and we can do this in prayer as well as in person.

Dr. Samuel Zwemer spent most of his life as a missionary in Arabia. When he was asked "Why?" his response usually ended with the words of Peter: "Master, we worked hard all night and caught nothing, but at your bidding I will let down the nets" (Luke 5:5). He believed that if we were obedient to Christ's commission, we too would see a great ingathering from the Muslim world.

The promises in the Word of God were enough for Samuel Zwemer, and they are enough for me. Knowing how God has answered prayer and done exceeding abundantly above all we have asked in Afghanistan, makes me believe that the Lord still has great things in store for the people of this central Asian nation.

There is much yet to take place in the story of God's work in this resistant land. The more men and women of dedication who set their sights on God's promises when they plow the "fields of Afghanistan," the faster this stubborn land will lose its label—"the forbidden harvest."

Chapter 3

The New Age Rage*

A "Missionary" Is Delivered of A Demon

For years I did not believe evil spirits or demons existed. I had grown up with the teaching that deliverance was not for today—it had ended with the first century Church. In the same way, the gifts of the Holy Spirit were no longer needed today, since the Church was "up and running"—like a Model-T Ford that had been pushed to get it started but was now operating on its own power.

But that all changed when I went to Afghanistan. There I came face to face with the enemy in spiritual warfare. And I saw what he was doing to Christians.

From that time on I have taken the offensive against Satan and his demons, even as Jesus Christ has commanded us to do.

The turning point came when I met a Christian woman, from California, who came to Afghanistan with her four teenagers, two boys and two girls. She claimed that the Lord had sent her there as a "missionary."

Although we were in Afghanistan as self-supporting witnesses or "tentmakers," we did not use the term "missionary." To the Afghans, this term has political connotations. It's like being a member of the CIA. Whenever Islamic armies conquered a people, they would force them to convert to Islam. So the Afghans assumed that when the British Empire

---

*The title of this chapter, "The New Age Rage" is used with acknoledgement and thanks to my good friend Karen Hoyt, ed. *The New Age Rage*, Fleming H. Revell Co., 1987.

colonized India, the missionaries were the religious arm of the military and would force people to become Christians.

As a result, we didn't call ourselves missionaries. Instead, I was known as a Christian pastor and a Christian teacher. Others were Christian doctors and nurses, engineers, and secretaries. That was fine. But no "missionaries" were allowed in the country.

Yet this American woman openly proclaimed she was a "missionary."

The American Embassy thought I had brought her over. But I did not even know her until she began attending our church and her four children took part in our young people's activities.

One day I asked her about her husband.

She told me the Lord had told her to come to Afghanistan, but her husband had refused to come with her. She claimed that the Bible said if you give up your home, your country, and your husband for Christ's' sake, He would reward you a hundred fold.

"But the Bible doesn't say that," I countered.

I turned to Mark 10:29 to read her the passage to show her that the Bible did not say she should leave her husband. Before I could, however, my eye first fell on Mark 9:29 which said: "This kind (of demon) comes out only by prayer." This was God warning me.

As I read Mark 10:29 to her, she became very upset. "Well, even though it isn't in the Bible," she said, "the Lord told me to leave my husband, and the Lord knows more than the Bible!"

When she said that, I knew she was on shaky ground! But she resisted all attempts to hear the truth, and became very angry, vowing that neither she nor her children would ever go to our church again.

Not long afterwards, however, she phoned me to say she was in terrible trouble. I asked a church elder, John Strachan of Scotland, to go with me to her home.

"I just received word that my husband, in the States, is divorcing me on grounds of desertion," she confided. "And I don't have any money to feed my children." All she had in the cupboard was a bag of rice. She had been cooking them rice for breakfast and rice for supper. The children skipped lunch completely. "I don't even have money to pay the rent," she said.

Then she told us of the old secondhand VW minibus which she had bought. It didn't even have a battery! She claimed that the Lord had told her that morning that the VW would start even without a battery. When she tried to start it, of course, the engine would not work, so she had called us.

"I'm not sure this is the Lord speaking to me after all," she said.

"How does the Lord speak to you?" I asked

"Through a Ouija board!"

Well! Then the story came out.

She had bought a Ouija board in California as a game for her family, and it began giving her "messages." It told her to sell her home and go to the animal pound where she would find a white dog. She was to bring the dog home and name him "Friend." Then she was to take the dog with her and go to Afghanistan, where she would find Jesus Christ living there as a little 7-year-old boy, having been born again on this earth. She was told to raise him and then to go with Jesus to Jerusalem to help him rebuild the Temple. She thought all these messages were from the Lord.

It was with this vision that she had come to Afghanistan.

"That is not the Lord speaking to you," I told her. "That is the Devil, who is the great Deceiver. The Lord takes care of His own when He calls them. But here your husband is divorcing you, and you don't have any food or money."

While we had been talking this way, her white dog had been jumping wildly against the door separating the two rooms.

"Look, we've got to get rid of these things," I told her.

She brought out the Ouija board, and we burned it right then and there in her fireplace.

I asked if she had anything else.

"Yes," she replied. "The Ouija board gave me the architectural drawings for the Temple in Jerusalem. I have all that."

"Those must be burned too. Is there anything else?"

"Oh yes, whenever the children get sick, I ask the Ouija board what medicine to give, and it gives me prescriptions."

"Let's get rid of those. Is there anything else?"

"I think the dog 'Friend' has something to do with it too."

Like the pigs at Gadara during our Lord's time, the dog was demon-possessed.

So John Strachan and I took the dog outside of Kabul into a valley where we shot him and then buried him.

Since I had never experienced anything like this before, I was in beyond my depth. I went to my library and read books on the occult.

At that time, we had been sending out a prayer letter every month. For the past several months, we had asked people for intercessory prayer about this whole situation. We knew we were in spiritual warfare, and that Satan was working through this woman to discredit the Lord's work. And God answered those prayers by sending us a Christian who knew exactly what to do.

We received word that a Mrs. Mitchell was coming to visit Afghanistan. She was a strong, deeply committed Christian, eighty-seven years old! All six of her children had become missionaries. Even some of her grandchildren were missionaries. Now she was traveling around the world visiting them on the mission field!

I met her at the airport the next morning.

"Mrs. Mitchell," I said. "God has brought you here just at the right time." And I described what was going on.

"Don't worry," she said. "The Lord will take care of it." She acted as if it were an everyday occurrence!

I took Mrs. Mitchell to the woman's home. As soon as we arrived, I knew things had grown worse. The woman was distraught. "Last night all hell broke loose in this house," she cried. "Whenever we would look at the sofa, it would sink down as if someone were sitting on it, although no one was around. Then pictures moved about on the walls. The furniture shifted and moved from one end of the room to the other, and even around the house. I went into one bedroom with my two daughters. My two sons were in the other bedroom. We couldn't sleep a wink all night because we sensed the presence of grotesque shapes, the presence of evil all around us. We also kept hearing blood-curdling screams. We were awake all night."

"Let's hold hands and form a circle," Mrs. Mitchell said with authority. We did so immediately.

"Now let's sing the Doxology." And we sang "Praise God From Whom All Blessings Flow."

After we finished singing, she turned to me. "Christy, would you lead in prayer?" So I did, and while I was praying, the woman fell down on the floor inside the circle.

Mrs. Mitchell interrupted my prayer and pointed her finger at her and said with authority, "In the name of Jesus Christ, come out! In the name of Jesus Christ, come out, and don't enter her or anyone else again!"

The lady got up.

"A demon just came out of me," she said.

We continued in prayer until the deliverance was complete. Then Mrs. Mitchell invited the woman and her four children to the Intercontinental Hotel for lunch because they were hungry.

I had already warned the U.S. Ambassador that there was an American there who wanted to rebuild the Temple in Jerusalem. I did this because years earlier a terrible international incident had developed when an Australian member of the Armstrong cult, the Worldwide Church of God, had gone to Jerusalem to burn down the Al Aksa mosque, in preparation for rebuilding the Temple. Muslims around the world had blamed the Jews for the incident. I didn't want a similar situation to develop now.

However, after the "missionary" was delivered of the demon of deceit, I told the American Ambassador what happened. He was amazed.

He then arranged for the entire family to fly back to New York City on the condition that they would repay their air fare later.

When the woman returned to the States, she immediately phoned her husband, seeking a reconciliation.

"Darling," he replied, "the only reason I wanted a divorce was because you left me. But since you've come back, I'm going to drop the whole thing." After they were reunited, I visited the family. I now believe that even Christians can be oppressed by demons. Some say demons can't enter Christians because the Holy Spirit dwells in us. Well, Christians get sick, don't they? Yet the Holy Spirit still dwells in us. Demon oppression is a spiritual sickness brought on by Satan through demonic deception and attack.

We must take the offensive against Satan and bind him. We must use the authority Jesus Christ has already given us. "All authority in heaven and on earth has been given to Me," He said. "Therefore *you* go and make disciples from among all nations. And these signs will follow you. Demons will come out ..." In the Lord's Prayer, He also taught us to ask the Father to "deliver us from the evil one."

Deliverance ministry in the Name of Jesus Christ is taking place all over the world today, including America.

Startled By An Angel

One look at the young man sitting in the Gordon-Conwell cafeteria and I knew he wasn't a student here. A pack of cigarettes lay prominently before him.

However, one of my students had brought us together, anxious that we should meet. And as I listened to the young Jewish man, whom we will call John, tell his story, I was amazed.

John's father owned optical stores in the Boston area and was well-to-do. When John was ten years old, he began taking drugs, and became a drug addict for the next fourteen years. Far more tragic, he became involved in Satan worship. In his bedroom at home (he lived with his parents), he set up an altar to the Devil. He stole neighborhood pets and sacrificed them to Satan.

Finally, the situation became so bad that his parents ordered him to leave home. Cut off from any funds, John needed two full-time jobs to support his drug habit. He worked from 8:00 a.m. to 4:00 p.m., and then from 5:00 p.m. to 1:00 a.m. He would sleep for a few hours in the bushes at a mall and then get up to go to work.

On weekends when John had time off, he would spend all his money on drugs. One time he overdosed, ending up in a hospital. After treating him, they sent him to a detoxification center.

There he met a Christian girl, whom we will call Mary, fell in love with her and wanted to marry her. But she said she couldn't marry him because the Bible says not to be unequally yoked with unbelievers.

"Tell me what I need to do, and I'll gladly do it." He was so much in love with her that he would do anything to marry her.

"You have to pray and ask the Lord to forgive your sins, and thank Jesus for being your Messiah. Thank Him for dying on the cross and shedding His blood for your sins, and rising from the dead. And ask Him to be your Savior."

"Fine, I'll do that," he said. And he did it just to please her.

The amazing thing was that the Lord answered him in a truly astonishing way.

By this time, John had been released from the drug rehab center, and his father and mother had received him back into their home.

One day John went to see Mary, now his fiancée. He was driving his father's Mercedes in the fast lane of a major highway.

Suddenly, from the corner of his eye, he saw a huge knee in the front seat next to him. He turned around and stared, for there beside him sat this huge man, much bigger than any ordinary person. He was so huge that he had to crouch down so as not to bump his head under the car roof. The stranger wore a beard and was dressed somewhat like John the Baptist! And he smelled wonderful—like the scent of new mown hay!

When John saw this, he was so startled that he almost crashed into the median strip! But then he pulled over into the breakdown lane and came to a full stop. As soon as he stopped the car, the man vanished.

It had been an angel!

When John picked up Mary later, he would not let her sit in front seat, afraid the angel might appear again.

The next morning, when he went to take his father's car out of the garage, he heard the Lord's voice, calling him by name.

"John, I want you to go into the woods and fast for three days and three nights. Furthermore, I want you to go to Gordon-Conwell." Although John lived near the Seminary, he had never been there. He said he avoided the place because he didn't want to have anything to do with religious people.

But because God spoke to him, he came to our campus.

"I'm here," he announced to a student when he arrived.

"What do you mean?" the other asked.

"God has sent me here."

The student then invited John to the cafeteria and that's when he introduced him to me.

I could see that John needed discipleship, so I invited him to my study and spent several hours with him. Since he didn't know anything about the Bible, I showed him how Christ had fulfilled the Scriptural prophecies about the Messiah. I explained the various steps in Christian growth, encouraging him to pray regularly, read his Bible every day, obey what he read in it, and tell others what Jesus had done for him.

Then, to help him grow in his faith, I invited John and his fiancée to our home where both Betty and I could disciple them.

Labor Day weekend was approaching, and my wife and I had planned to go to an International Student Conference in the Berkshires over that holiday weekend in 1990. I told John and Mary we would have to be away that weekend and would not be able to meet with them. Suddenly a thought came to me. "Would you like to go with us?" I asked them.

"Oh, we'd love to!" they replied. So I phoned the conference center and asked if they had room for two more.

"Sorry," came the reply. "We're completely booked. Every bed is taken. We don't even have room for one more person."

"I'm so sorry to hear that," I said, "because there's this young Jewish man who recently became a Christian, and he and his fiancée have their hearts set on going."

"Give us twenty minutes," they replied. "Then call us back. We'll see if there's anything we can do." During those twenty minutes, Betty and I prayed with John and Mary that if it were God's will for them to go, then a way would open up.

I called back in twenty minutes.

"If this couple doesn't mind sleeping on roll-away beds, then we can set one up in the men's dorm and another in the women's dorm. We can accommodate them."

"I'm sure they won't mind," I assured them, knowing that John had slept in the bushes. Roll-away beds would be just fine.

So the conference center took their reservations, and Betty and I drove up with them on a Friday afternoon.

When we arrived at Hephzibah Heights and I saw the beautiful wooded grounds surrounded by hills, I suddenly remembered what the

Lord had told John to do! The Lord had told him to spend three days and three nights in the woods fasting.

"John," I said. "This is the fasting the Lord told you to do. There are many kinds of fasting. Since you are a chain-smoker, when you give up smoking, you will be fasting for the Lord." He was thrilled. Having read in the conference brochure that no smoking was allowed in the buildings or grounds, John had already decided he wouldn't smoke for the three days he was there.

"That's right," he reminisced. "That is what God told me to do."

We had a wonderful time together, and both John and Mary were strengthened by the Christian fellowship and the messages given by the speakers. He and Mary finally got married, and I was asked to take part in the ceremony. Today they have a little girl.

John was baptized in December 1990. He has been working with his father in the optical business. In fact, he gave me a new pair of glasses. They're trifocals (for working at the computer) and are treated to filter out harmful ultraviolet rays at high altitudes, because he knew we would be returning to Afghanistan.

Please pray for this couple. I know God can use them.

Escape From the New Age

Donna Hailson, one of my students at Gordon-Conwell, formerly taught in a public high school in Massachusetts. She was asked by the administration to teach the literature of the occult and yoga.

Not only would she hypnotize her entire class but she also used to lead them in regressive experiences to discover their past lives. She also had real witches come and speak to the class. No parent or anyone else objected. Outside of school, she used Ouija boards and tarot cards, and read palms and tea leaves. She was a medium through whom other worldly spirits would speak. She also prepared horoscopes for people based on the stars. Imagine, how can a star rule your life! Ridiculous! It's just like crystals. What can a stone do? You're not worshiping stars or stones. You're really worshiping demons.

All this time some Christian friends were praying for her. It was the week of the Billy Graham Crusade in Boston in 1982, and they invited her to go with them. She accepted. The weather was terrible—it was raining and blowing although it was June. But this was God's time for her. She went forward and received Christ as her Savior.

Then she invited her husband Gene to go with her the following night. "You must come and hear this man Billy Graham," she said.

The next night he went with her to the Crusade and this time *he* went forward to receive Christ as his Savior. Donna also led her daughter Brooke to the Lord.

Donna came to Gordon-Conwell and graduated in May 1990. She was my teaching assistant. She now has her Master of Divinity degree. She receives many invitations to speak on the New Age Movement and has started an organization called Evangel Ministries. No one can argue with her about the occult and what its effects are because she was once involved in it and she knows it as only an insider can. She speaks from experience.

Today, Donna is pastoring a church in New Hampshire while working on her Ph.D. from the University of Sterling in Scotland and is writing her thesis on the deception of New Age goddesses. She is a gifted woman of God. Recently she shared her testimony coast to coast on Billy Graham's television broadcast.

The Rich Young Sikh Who Followed Jesus

Bakht Singh was a Sikh, born into a wealthy Indian family in the north of India. Yet he left everything behind to follow Jesus. And the Lord has used him to plant more than 600 churches, all self-supporting, in India, Pakistan, Nepal, and Sri Lanka.

As a young man, Bakht Singh went abroad to England, where he studied agricultural engineering. There, embarrassed by his long hair, he had his first hair cut. (Sikh men are never supposed to cut their hair—that's why they wear large turbans.)

After completing his studies in England, he went to Canada to gain the practical experience he needed.

On board the British liner bound for Canada, Bakht Singh wanted to show the others that he was just as good as they were, even though he did have dark skin. So he attended all the dances and took part in all the hobby horse races they conducted.

He also attended the Sunday morning Anglican church service, for the same reason. "I'm just as good as anyone else," he thought to himself. "So I can go to their church service."

As Bakht Singh sat in the ship's lounge, waiting for the worship service to begin, the Captain arrived. Immediately everyone knelt in worship.

"I'm not going to kneel to the Christian God," Bakht Singh thought to himself. So he planned to get up and leave.

But there were people kneeling in front of him, on both sides of him, and behind him. He was trapped. Rather than create a commotion, he decided to stay.

"Oh well," he figured. "It won't hurt me to kneel." So he too knelt. But as soon as he fell to his knees, he realized he was kneeling before Jesus Christ, and he sensed Christ's presence and power!

This began Bakht Singh's search to know the Living Christ.

When he arrived in Canada, he went to a church for the first time in his life. But the people had such long, sad faces that he was sure they didn't have the answers to life. So Bakht Singh decided to go to church when no one was there and just meditate.

While he was staying in the YMCA in Winnipeg, Manitoba, Bakht Singh heard a young man singing in the shower.

"Here I am lonely and sad," he thought. "And this man is so happy and joyful. I wonder why? As soon as he gets out of the shower, I'm going to ask him." And that's exactly what he did.

"I'm happy," the young man told Bakht Singh, "because all my sins are forgiven. I have everlasting life. I know Jesus Christ as my personal Savior and Lord."

"Tell me more," Bakht Singh pleaded. So the young man told him about Jesus. Realizing that Bakht Singh was hungering and thirsting for more, the young man gave him his own Bible. "Here, you may borrow my Bible. It will answer your questions."

So hungry was he for the truth that Bakht Singh sat up all night reading through the Gospels of Matthew, Mark, Luke, and into John. At first he thought this was a holy book for Westerners only—until he read in John: "Behold, the Lamb of God who takes away the sin of the world!" *The sin of the world—not the sin of the West!* Suddenly Bakht Singh realized this included him.

Then he read in John 3:16 that "God so loved the world *(not just the West)* that He gave His only begotten Son, that whosoever believes in Him should not perish but have everlasting life. For God did not send His Son into *the world* to condemn *the world*, but that through Him *the world* might be saved." He had never heard that before! Since he had just read what Jesus said to Nicodemus about being born again, Bakht Singh knelt down beside his bed and asked the Lord to forgive his sins and to give him a new life. And Christ did. From that moment on, Bakht Singh's life was changed.

At first, he planned to return to India and make a lot of money to use for the Lord's work. But the Lord spoke to him.

"I don't want your money, I want you!"

Like Moses, he resisted.

"Lord, I can't speak." (He had a speech impediment.)

"If I made your mouth, can I not make you speak?" the Lord replied.

Finally Bakht Singh surrendered. Shortly after, he attended a church service where the speaker was Dr. Clarence Jones, a missionary to South America who had helped launch the Christian radio broadcasts over HCJB in Quito, Ecuador. This was the first missionary-run radio station in the the world.

"We're so happy to have a guest from India here tonight who is going to share his testimony," the leader told the group. Bakht Singh looked around the church to see who this guest was from India. Then he heard the leader say, "It's Bakht Singh!" This caught him off guard. He had not known they were going to call on him. Although he felt very nervous, he gave his testimony of how he had come to Christ.

Before Bakht Singh returned to India, he wrote and told his family that he had accepted Christ as his Lord and Savior.

When he was reunited with his family in Bombay, his father said: "We received your letter. We know you have become a Christian. We will be happy to let you come home with us on one condition: that you never mention this to a single soul. The family honor is at stake. We will all be disgraced if anyone finds out."

Because he loved his father and mother and wife so deeply, Bakht Singh was tempted to agree. But then he remembered the words of Jesus Christ: "If anyone loves father or mother or wife ... more than Me, he is not worthy of Me."

"I love you," Bakht Singh told his father and mother and his wife. "But Jesus is my God. He has created me and He has saved me. He has forgiven me and given me everlasting life. I'm afraid I can't agree to keep quiet about Him."

So his father disowned him. His parents and his wife left him. He never married again. However, many years later, he did have the privilege of baptizing his parents.

Although Bakht Singh had no money, he was filled with joy. He would witness to people on the streets of Bombay about Christ, and they would invite him to a meal or a cup of tea in a restaurant.

One time he had gone all day without having even a cup of tea. He was hungry when he went to bed. In the middle of the night he heard someone knocking on his door. Getting up, he dressed and went to see who was there. A man stood outside, a total stranger.

"Is there anyone here by the name of Bakht Singh?" the stranger asked.

"Yes, I'm Bakht Singh."

"I had a dream tonight," the man explained. "Jesus Christ appeared to me. He told me to come to this address and find someone by the name of Bakht Singh and invite him to dinner." So Bakht Singh went with him.

"What a wonderful dinner this man cooked for me," he told me later, "because Jesus had told him to do it!"

For the next three years Bakht Singh did nothing but study the Scriptures. He read the whole Bible through more than a hundred times! I have never met anyone who knows the Scriptures as well as he does. Every letter he writes includes Bible references which serve as a sermon.

I came to know Bakht Singh when he came to Toronto as one of the main speakers for the first InterVarsity Missionary Convention in December 1946, where I also met my wife Betty. I remember how he slipped on the ice and broke his right arm with a compound fracture. We rushed him to the hospital where the doctors had X-rays taken.

"Your arm is broken so badly," the doctors told him, "that we'll have to open it up and reset the broken bones."

"Well, can I speak at the Convention?" Bakht Singh asked.

"Absolutely not," they replied. "You'll be in the hospital for weeks."

"Can you wait until after I speak?" he asked them. "Then I'll come in for the operation." The doctors consulted with each other.

"It's your arm," they finally concluded. "You'll be in terrible pain. But if that's the way you want it, medically speaking, it will be all right." So they set his arm in a sling, and he went on to speak, as scheduled.

Was he powerful! He spoke on counting the cost of following Jesus. It was based on Luke 14 where Jesus says: "No one builds a tower without first counting the cost ... "

"Young people," he said, "count the cost of following Jesus. Don't follow him lightly." Bakht Singh knew the Bible so well that he could hold it open in one hand and quote from it extensively, without even glancing at it. He was a tremendous blessing!

One of the students at the Convention asked him, "Brother Bakht Singh, if you're a man of God, why did He let you slip and fall and break your arm?"

"Well, I don't know all the reasons," Bakht Singh replied. "But I do know one thing: ever since it happened, I have been in such pain that I haven't been able to sleep a wink. This has kept me awake so that I could pray without ceasing for you young people."

After Bakht Singh finished his talk, we rushed him to the hospital where they performed surgery on his arm. I visited him there daily. Sharing his hospital room was a Canadian businessman, a nominal Christian. So Bakht Singh told the businessman the following story.

"I come from India where we grow tea. We exported it to the British Isles where they put it in fancy boxes and shipped it all over the world. But even though we grew and exported tea, we never drank it ourselves. We never even tasted it! Finally we became curious. If other people liked the tea so much, we should try it too. We did, and it was so good that we've been drinking tea ever since!

"You Canadians have also been exporting a wonderful product—the Lord Jesus Christ—to the rest of the world through your missionaries. Now I've come to tell you to 'taste and see that the Lord is good. Happy is the man who puts his trust in Him.'" And then he led the businessman to Christ!

This businessman became so excited that when his family came to visit, he had Bakht Singh witness to them as well. His hospital room was soon turned into an evangelistic center. When I went to see him, it was filled with doctors, nurses, paramedics, and patients from up and down the hall. There was Bakht Singh in the midst of them, preaching in his hospital room! And all these people were fascinated with what he was sharing.

An Indian Hindu student, studying for his Ph.D. in atomic science at the University of Toronto, had heard about Bakht Singh and his conversion to Christ. He wanted to straighten him out so he asked me to introduce them.

As soon as we arrived at the hospital room, I told Bakht Singh this young student had some questions for him.

"Before we talk," said Bakht Singh, "let's ask the Lord to guide our conversation." And he made this Ph.D. student get down on his knees there in the hospital room! "Dear Lord, this friend from India has come with questions. Help us to answer them because You are all-wise. You know everything and You want us to understand Your truth. In Jesus' name, Amen."

Well, this young Ph.D. student became so flustered when Bakht Singh led him in prayer that he forgot all his questions! He was speechless. He didn't know what to say. So Bakht Singh then began to witness to him, telling him how he had found true forgiveness and peace in Jesus Christ.

Years later when Bakht Singh visited us in Kabul, Afghanistan, I asked him to lead the devotions at breakfast. He looked up at the beautiful snow-capped mountains surrounding Kabul and spoke:

"Let us reflect on 'the mountain peaks' in the book of Isaiah," he began. And then by memory, he quoted the key verse in each of the sixty-six chapters of the book of Isaiah. That was his devotional!

Today, Bakht Singh is a very old man, nearly ninety. He counted the cost and decided to follow Jesus. The Lord has used him in a mighty way.

The Tree Dwellers

USAID hired a forestry expert from America to come to Afghanistan and show the people how to plant trees. Most of the mountains in Afghanistan are without forestation. Trees would not only provide the wood the people need, but trees bearing nuts or fruit would also provide nutritious food. In fact, trees would produce greater rainfall than lakes because so much evaporation takes place through the leaves.

The tamarisk tree—which Abraham planted in Beersheba (Genesis 21:33)—was the best choice for Afghanistan, the expert concluded. Afghanistan should plant millions of these trees. Why? Because the tamarisk tree gets its moisture from the air! It doesn't need much water but can grow very well in dry, desert areas. So he grew millions of saplings for the Afghans.

All this was very scientific. But the Afghans refused to go along with him.

Frustrated, the American asked me, "Why, don't the Afghans want to plant these trees?" Lacking an answer, I asked one of the nationals outright.

"It's very simple," the Afghan replied. "We believe that demons roost in the branches of the tamarisk tree. So we plant these trees only in cemeteries, where no one goes at night. If we planted them all over Afghanistan, we would be inviting these demons to dwell close to our houses, in our gardens, and along our roads, and they would cause great harm."

So they refused to plant these trees. Their fear of evil spirits far outweighed the agricultural and economic benefits of the trees. They considered themselves good Muslims, but cases like this prove that "popular" or folk Islam is chiefly animistic.

Doorways for Demons

I remember what a shock it was the first time I went to India and saw those hideous idols in the temples, with well-dressed people bowing low and worshiping them.

The Bible calls this demon worship!

The Bible says that people who worship such idols are not merely worshiping idols of wood, stone, and metal, but they are actually worshiping demons! The Apostle Paul writes about this in I Corinthians 10:20, "The sacrifices of pagans are offered to demons, not to God, and I don't want you to be participants with demons."

Yet unwittingly, American tourists overseas will buy replicas of these idols and display them in their home. Unknown to them, they are actually introducing demons into their homes!

Tragically, most Christians don't realize this even though the Bible says, "Do not bring an idol into your home" (Deuteronomy 7:26).

When we were in Afghanistan, a Muslim presented me with a bronze idol. He thought I would like it as a souvenir. As soon as he left, I burned the thing! We had a huge pot-belly coal stove, U.S. Army surplus, which quickly melted the idol down.

Another time, a hippie oppressed with demons gave me his Satanic records. "I want to get rid of these," he said. I took them and burned them at once in that same stove.

Later on, he wanted them back. When he found out that I had burned them, he told me I had done the right thing.

Satan uses these things to get a foothold in our lives. It's crucial that we slam the door on demons. Remember how Moses melted the golden calf idol which the children of Israel had made. Then he ground it into powder and threw it into the water, making them drink it to teach them a lesson.

The 13th Floor and Other Superstitions

When Dr. Samuel Zwemer, that great missionary to the Muslims, retired from teaching missions at Princeton Seminary, he went to live in New York City. There he rented an apartment right on Fifth Avenue for a very low price. Do you know how he did it? He rented a suite on the thirteenth floor of the apartment building! No one else would live there.

I visited him at home, and in the elevator the floors were marked "12 ... 12A ... 14 ..." Even though they called the floor 12A, still no one would rent a room there. Being superstitious, they were afraid of the thirteenth floor! Well, we may call that superstition, but it's actually a form of animism—to be afraid of numbers!

We see many athletes using animistic fetishes for good luck. I remember the football coach at Princeton University. He belonged to the Phi Beta Kappa honors society and was a brilliant man. Yet he would always wear the same old pair of pants to every game because he felt that it would bring his team good luck. What can an old pair of pants do to help you win a football game?

If you watch big league baseball games, you'll notice when the coach comes to relieve the pitcher, even though he looks so tough, he will dance around the baselines. He thinks that if he steps on any of those white lines, it will bring bad luck to his team.

Often people will make a remark and then quickly add, "Knock on wood." Well, that's pure animism. What does knocking on wood accomplish? You're attributing some sort of power to wood.

Then there's the expression, "You can thank your lucky stars." Well, the stars aren't lucky. In fact, even Shakespeare knew that, because in his play *Julius Caesar* he has Cassius say, "It is not in our stars but in ourselves that we are underlings."

Many people won't walk under a ladder because they fear it will bring bad luck. In a sense, that's a good idea if someone's painting up there!

When someone sneezes, people say, "God bless you." Well, that's animistic too. Animists believe that when you sneeze, there's a danger that your spirit may leave your body. And so by blessing you with a perfunctory prayer, they prevent that from happening. You hear many Christians say, *"Gesundheit"* or "God bless you" without realizing that this is animism!

Also in the States, you'll often see barns with cupolas or spires on the roofs. They're built to look like a church. I've even seen barns with Gothic windows painted on them. This is all done to fool the spirits of lightning and fire! Some think that if evil spirits see a church, they'll be afraid of it, whereas they would more readily attack a barn. That's why you have hex signs painted on barns and even homes, to protect them against evil spirits.

From the well-known children's story "The Three Little Pigs," we have expressions like, "Not by the hair of my chinny chin-chin will I let you in!" That is swearing by the hair on your chin! Hair is often associated with animism because animists believe that hair is the seat of soul stuff.

An interesting story shows the importance of hair in animistic religions, like Folk Islam, as practiced daily by the people. When my wife and I first arrived in Afghanistan, a solidly Muslim country, an Afghan had just returned from a pilgrimage to Mecca, where he had purchased what was claimed to be one of the Prophet Mohammed's hairs. He had paid a great deal of money for this single hair.

The news of this "sacred" hair created quite a stir in the country. The Jalalabad area had received a government grant to build a boys' school. Now, instead, they took the money and put up a huge shrine to this hair!

A newspaper editor in Kabul wrote an editorial protesting that even if this were a hair of Mohammed, Mohammed himself would not want to take money away from a school for Muslim boys and use it instead to build a shrine for one of his hairs! Furthermore, he added, we have no guarantee that this is actually Mohammed's hair. It might be the hair of a donkey, for all he knew!

When this article appeared, tempers really flared! The priests in the country were divided into two groups. One group wanted to kill this newspaper editor. The other said, "No. He's right. It's wrong to divert the money from education and use it for this hair."

To calm the situation, the government appointed the editor as an ambassador, just to get him out of the country. And they did build the shrine to that hair of Mohammed!

The Demons Are Migrating North

Don Richardson, author of the missionary best-sellers *Peace Child* and *Eternity in Their Hearts*, once observed that that there are more Christians today south of the equator than there are north of it—because great masses of people have been coming to Christ in Africa, Latin America, and Oceania.

He believes that, as a result, most of the evil spirits have migrated to the northern hemisphere. That explains the revival of the occult and the rise of the New Age Movement in America and Europe. It reminds me of the time when Christ cast out the demons from the Gadarene demoniac, and the demons asked Him to let them enter the pigs. Thus they migrated from the demon-possessed man into the animals.

We do have a revival of the occult in the West. We really need to pray that the Lord will reach those in the occult, deliver them, and bring them to Christ.

Although the Bible says that the whole world will be evangelized one day, the majority of people will not be Christian.

Jesus said: "Broad is the gate that leads to destruction, and many enter through it. But small is the gate and narrow is the road that leads to life, and only a few find it." According to the Bible then, real believers will be a minority.

Dr. Adoniram Judson Gordon used to say that the matter of evangelization is not to bring the whole world to Christ, but to bring Christ to the whole world.

The Futility of Ancestor Worship

Dr. Kinston Keh was the president of a national silk company in China. When the Communists took over, he went to Afghanistan, where he served with the United Nations in developing the silk industry. He was a brilliant agriculturist. *(For more on Dr. Keh, see the story "Silkworms, Trout, and Ducklings" in Chapter 6.)*

Dr. Keh was also an elder in our church in Kabul. His wife, however, was a Buddhist.

"Why don't you read your Bible more?" she asked him one day. "You're a Christian. You should study your Scriptures."

"You know I'm busy from morning till night with my work," he answered.

"Well, you're a Christian," she said. "You should know your Bible better. I tell you what. I'll read it for you. While you're eating breakfast, lunch, and dinner, I'll tell you what I've read."

She read through the whole Bible three-and-a-half times. As a result, she received Jesus Christ as her Savior! She became a wonderful Christian, and I had the privilege of baptizing her in Kabul.

A few months after this, she died very suddenly of a cerebral hemorrhage. After her funeral, Dr. Keh came to me. Since he was still influenced by the common practice of "ancestor worship" in China, he asked me, "Will you please pray for my wife?"

"Well, Dr. Keh, what would you like me to pray? Shall I pray that her sins be forgiven?"

"Oh, no," he replied. "She received Jesus Christ as her Savior. Through His blood, all her sins are forgiven."

"Well, shall I pray that she'll be happy?" I asked.

"Oh, no. The Bible says that in God's presence there is fullness of joy."

"Well, shall I pray that she'll have enough things—enough to eat and wear?"

"Oh, no. She doesn't need that."

"Then what do you want me to pray for?"

There was a long pause. "Oh, I see," said Dr. Keh. "You don't need to pray for her. Pray for me." I gladly did this for him.

Friday the Thirteenth

Christians who allow superstitions like Friday the Thirteenth to affect their thinking are giving Satan a foothold to enter their lives. Such fears are nothing but animism which has crept into our own culture. We need to claim the Lord's power over animism, which ascribes powers to inanimate things.

I'll never forget an experience I had.

Once when I was back from Afghanistan, I went deep sea fishing with my younger brother Stanley off the coast of California. On the drive down there, I read him the accounts in the Bible where Christ helped the disciples catch huge numbers of fish. I prayed that the same Lord would help us since Stan loved sports so much.

When our boat had pulled away from the dock at Princeton By the Sea, the captain said, "I'm afraid the fishing isn't going to be good today because it's Friday the thirteenth." He probably didn't say it earlier because he didn't want to lose customers.

I prayed the Lord would confound his counsel. And He did.

We caught all kinds of fish. We went through school after school and we just kept reeling the fish in as fast as we could!

When we arrived home, we had such a large catch that we had no place to store all the fish. So we spread them out on my brother's lawn.

All the kids from the neighborhood soon piled into the yard. Rather than clean all that fish himself, my brother gave the fish away to the kids to take home to their mothers so *they* would clean them!

We had caught all that fish because the Lord overcame Friday the thirteenth!

By contrast, when we fear something, it gives Satan a chance to get in through our defenses. This is what I think happened to Job.

"That which I feared has happened unto me," Job said. Job allowed his worst fears to get the better of him, instead of placing his trust completely in the Lord.

Through animism, Satan can also attack Christians who are not alert and who do not stand guard against his scheming.

The Hungry Fish

Besides controlling much of the fishing industry in Gloucester, Massachusetts, the Unification Church or "Moonies," as they are known, have had twelve of their members enrolled at Harvard Divinity School in Cambridge.

We met with these twelve Unification Church members one Saturday at their invitation for a discussion on theology.

Gordon-Conwell was invited to send twelve students and two faculty members. Someone accepted the invitation for me before I had a chance to turn it down. So Dr. Richard Lovelace and I accompanied the students to the one-day conference.

It was very interesting. A professor from the Unification Church School of Theology, in Tarrytown, New York, and another church leader represented the Moonies.

Because they said there would not be enough time for everyone to speak, they only allowed two students from Gordon-Conwell and two Moonies from Harvard Divinity School to give their testimonies.

Then they had the professor from the Unification Church summarize Mr. Moon's theology, and asked me to highlight evangelical theology. The discussion concluded with final remarks made by the Unification Church leader and by Professor Lovelace.

Dr. Lovelace, who comes up with amazing illustrations, made a very interesting analogy.

"I've been deeply impressed by the sincerity of you young people in the Unification Church who are studying at Harvard Divinity School. However, even though you are sincere, I must share a story which applies to you.

"There was a hungry fish out in the ocean, dreaming of finding a fat minnow to swallow. As it was swimming along, it saw a shiny minnow flash by and grabbed it—only to discover that the minnow was a lure and had hooks in it.

"The hungry fish was caught!

"This is what has happened to you. You have been after real spiritual food, but you've been hooked by an artificial lure. You have been caught by this false system."

The Moonies sat there in stunned silence. They could not help but see the point.

Chapter 4

The Collapse of Communism

The Courageous Pastor of Romania

Dr. Josef Tson is a former Communist who became a Christian. He escaped from Romania and went to England, where he received his Master of Divinity degree at Oxford University. After completing this degree, he wanted to return to Romania as a Christian pastor.

"Don't do that. You'll be killed," many Christian friends urged.

"Look, Jesus Christ was killed," was his reply.

He studied his Bible to see where the Lord wanted to lead him and came to understand the teaching of willingly suffering for Christ—even as Christ Himself had suffered as the Lamb of God.

When he returned to Romania, he became pastor of a very large church in Oradea. As he watched the Communists trying to stamp out Christianity, he was moved to write the *Christian Manifesto*, criticizing the Communist repression. Although he knew it meant almost certain death, he published it nevertheless.

Almost immediately, Dr. Tson was arrested and his whole library was confiscated by the secret police.

He was interrogated every day from 8:00 a.m. to 4:00 p.m. and then allowed to return home. On evenings and weekends he was free to preach.

One day after an especially fruitless interrogation, the colonel in charge threatened: "Don't you realize I have the power to kill you?"

"Yes, I realize that," Dr. Tson replied. "But do you realize that I have the power to die?"

"What do you mean?" asked the Colonel.

"You can kill me," replied Dr. Tson, "but then my blood will cover my tapes, my messages, and all the books I have written. And my Christian witness will be ten times more effective."

"Go home!" growled the angry Colonel.

One Wednesday morning, Dr. Tson arrived as usual for his daily interrogation. His mind was filled with thoughts of that evening's Bible study, a teaching he wanted to prepare on the Holy Spirit. He desperately needed one book in particular on the Holy Spirit, but it was among the books the Communists had confiscated.

Suddenly, the Colonel interrupted his questioning to remark:

"By the way, I have an important meeting this morning from 9:00 a.m. until noon. Wait right here in my office until I return. So you won't be bored ..." And he leaned back and pulled out a book from the hundreds of volumes confiscated from Dr. Tson's library. He handed the book to Dr. Tson and said, "Here, read this."

It was the very book that he needed on the Holy Spirit!

Out of his entire library, this was the one he wanted for that night's Bible study! So for the next three hours, Dr. Tson took notes and prepared his message. God's providence was certainly in control of all events.

Interestingly enough, copies of Dr. Tson's *Christian Manifesto* eventually reached England, where it was translated into English. The English translation even found its way to Washington, D.C., at the very time when President Ceausescu was seeking favored-nation status for Romania so that he could receive economic aid from the United States. America would only give this aid to nations that lived up to the Helsinki agreement on human rights.

American officials presented President Ceausescu with the *Christian Manifesto*, saying, "Look, you don't have freedom of religion in Romania, so we can't give you favored-nation status."

"Release Dr. Tson!" Ceausescu immediately ordered his staff back in Romania. "We need to change this policy so that we can obtain economic aid."

After having interrogated Dr. Tson for six months, the Communists immediately let him go.

Dr. Tson was given the opportunity to leave Romania, and he came to the United States around 1981. Every single week since then, he has been broadcasting sermons to Romania. He told me that seven to eleven million Romanians listen to him regularly. Although it grieved him to leave his country, he had prepared the hearts of his people for the time when they would eventually overthrow the Communist régime.

For several years, Dr. Tson sponsored a secret underground seminary in Romania that has trained hundreds of pastors.

Seminary professors went to Romania for two weeks as tourists, visiting one of the many hot mineral springs in the country. There, instead of bathing in the medicinal waters, they would receive instructions on where to go next.

For example: "Take a walk out to such-and-such a place, and under a lamp post you will see a person who's wearing a black hat (or carrying a book). Follow that person."

When the professor arrived at his destination, he would find more than a hundred pastors gathered there, eager to learn. Later that night the professor would return to his hotel. For two weeks they would teach this way.

Without doubt, it was Dr. Josef Tson, along with other devoted Christians, who in many ways prepared the way for the overthrow of the Communist régime in Romania.

Ceausescu's evil government finally fell because of one Reformed pastor, Lazlo Tokos, who stood for the truth. The authorities sent the secret police to arrest him. But more than a hundred of Pastor Tokos' people came and supported him! They shouted: "If you're going to arrest the pastor, you'll have to arrest us all!"

Thousands of people then gathered in the main city square of Timisoara. Another pastor led all the people in the Lord's Prayer, as they fell to their knees on the cold ground.

Finally the Communist régime was forced to collapse in Romania.

Angels Guarding Beijing

Not long after the Tienemen Square massacre in Beijing, a friend of ours who had witnessed this tragedy came to Gordon-Conwell. His name is Dwyatt Gantt, and the organization he founded sends tentmakers to China.

As a fifty-year old pastor, Dwyatt had first gone to China with his wife in 1982 to teach English with ELIC, the English Language Institute of China.

He had prayed that the Lord would make that year the best year of his life. (Later he said, "God made that year better than my whole life!")

He told us of their initial impressions when they first arrived. They had been told they would have an apartment, but when they got there, they found only one small room! The room was freshly painted but the red paint was still wet. The bed was uncomfortable. And there was only one rickety chair.

"Lord," he thought, "is this what you brought me to China for?"

Then, although he didn't hear a voice, he felt the Lord speaking to him: "Dwyatt, I didn't bring you here for your comfort. I brought you here to comfort the Chinese." And how God has blessed him since! He went on to found University Language Services in China, which now has more than 600 tentmakers working there.

Dwyatt told us that he was in Beijing when the Tienemen Square massacre took place. On the night of the massacre, he had taken a taxi through Tienemen Square to return to his hotel. However, so preoccupied was he with his own problems that although he saw truckloads of armed soldiers, he didn't grasp the full import of what it might mean.

The next morning he heard the shocking news of the bloodbath. He personally knew students who had been there that night.

Overwhelmed with guilt and remorse at his insensitivity, he fell to his knees weeping, and asked God to forgive him.

"I'm not the kind of person who sees visions or angels," he told us later, "but as I was on my knees, praying and crying out to God, I looked out my hotel window and saw the heavens open up and two mighty angels of God appear. They were so powerful that one look at them and you knew that *nothing* could ever come against them!

"As the angels descended over Beijing, I recalled the words of Jesus Christ in Revelation: 'When I open the door, no one can close it.' I realized that in spite of Tienemen Square, China was not going to be closed to Christians!"

That very fall he came to Gordon-Conwell and recruited two of our students to go to Beijing.

"God is working in China and nothing can stop Him!" he told us.

A Communist Official Comes to Christ

A Chinese Communist official was sent to the United States for one year to study Christianity in America and to write an official report on it for his government. The Communists have been baffled by the Christian movement in China and wanted to understand it. During that year, this official visited many Christian centers across the country.

Now the Chinese think of America as a Christian country. But they don't really understand what that all means. They equate Christianity with democracy.

I first heard about this Communist official from Dr. Arthur Glasser, who had been a missionary to China before serving as Dean of the School of World Mission at Fuller Seminary in Pasadena, California. One afternoon Dr. Glasser phoned me, asking if the Chinese official could visit us. He had seen Fuller in Pasadena and now he needed to see "the Fuller of the East Coast—Gordon-Conwell." I told him we would be happy to welcome him.

The next Sunday morning the Communist official turned up at the first Presbyterian Church in Cambridge, Massachusetts, where I was preaching! After that service had ended at noon, I immediately took him with me to the Dorchester Christian Fellowship, which was made up mainly of poor people.

The Chinese official was amazed. He said he had never seen poor white people in a church before. He listened attentively to their testimonies of what Christ was doing currently in their lives.

"This church is the grass roots of Christianity!" he exclaimed.

After the service, we held a missions meeting in John and Kristen Ensor's home. John is a graduate of Gordon-Conwell. He and his wife are carrying on a marvelous ministry in the inner city.

"This is the first house church I've ever seen!" the Chinese official told me. In China, the house churches meet in secret, careful to avoid the scrutiny of government officials. So understandably, he was very excited about what he had seen and experienced.

By the end of the afternoon, we were quite hungry. We had had very little to eat between services since we barely had one hour to get from one church to the other.

"Wouldn't it be wonderful to give our guest a good Chinese dinner?" I thought.

So I took him and Barbara Yandell, a student who was driving us, to Wei-Lu's Restaurant on Route One. He loved it! The waiters and waitresses spoke to him in Mandarin. And the menu was in Chinese as well as English so he could understand it. We had a delicious meal.

That night, the official stayed over at our apartment on campus and, the following day, he visited at Gordon-Conwell.

I took him to the noonday missions prayer meeting. "Now, you're going to see students praying," I told him. "They meet every day for this. You won't have to pray, but since you're studying Christianity, I want you to come." He was very interested in the prayer meeting. Then he talked with our Chinese students. Some of them spent several hours with him. They were thrilled with the opportunity because he knew what the

Communist government had been doing in China. It was a revelation for them.

That evening the official attended my missions class.

During the break, I introduced him to George Kharlov, a new student from Russia, whose wife is Latvian. When the Communist official found out we had a student from Russia, he was astounded! You should have seen his face!

Then George put his hand on the man's shoulder and said to him, "God is doing great things in our two countries!" Well, that was the crowning touch. The official was at a loss for words!

The next day we showed him the video *Chariots of Fire*. I told him the story of Eric Liddell, the great Olympic champion born in China who later returned there as a missionary and died in a Japanese concentration camp. The Communist official was thrilled with the story.

When the time came for him to leave, we took him to the train station. While we waited, I told him the wonderful story of Charles Soong of the Soong dynasty, who met Christ in America and then returned to China, where he and his family rose to prominence *(see "From Tea Shop to National Leadership" in this chapter)*. One daughter married Sun Yat-sen, the first President of China, and also became Vice President of Communist China.

Before returning to China, this Communist official—who came to the States to study Christianity—made a decision to receive Jesus Christ as his personal Savior!

The Day Communism Began To Crumble

When the Soviet Union invaded Afghanistan on Christmas Day in 1979, it proved to be her greatest undoing. For in light of recent history, I believe it marked a watershed. It signaled the beginning of the end for Communism throughout Eastern Europe and the rest of the world.

That Christmas Day also marked the beginning of daily prayer for Afghanistan's freedom, intercession that was dramatically answered ten years later when Russia withdrew from Afghanistan, on February 15, 1989.

Ten years earlier, however, in December 1979, the United States had focused its attention on gaining the release of the American hostages taken captive from the U.S. Embassy in Tehran. So while President Jimmy Carter and the State Department were dealing with the Ayatollah Khomeini and Iran, Russia pulled a fast one. Breshnev was certain they could conquer Afghanistan in a few days. This would put them close to gaining a warm-water port through Baluchistan in western Pakistan.

Then President Carter told the Soviet Union that if she went any farther into Pakistan, that would launch World War III. Yet in stating that, he was, in effect, handing over Afghanistan to Russia as a *fait accompli*.

Few realized at the time what fighters the Afghans were.

As the Russian army swept across Afghanistan, more than five million Afghans began their exodus from their homeland, rather than live under Communism. My wife and I watched the television news coverage, our hearts breaking at the devastation and the millions of refugees streaming into Pakistan and Iran. Most of these refugees were children, little boys and girls!

"Oh, how I would love to go and help those refugees! We know their language, we could do something," I said to Betty.

Within a couple of days, our phone rang. It was the Christian evangelical relief agency called World Concern.

"We want to help the Afghan refugees," they said. "But we don't want the relief to get into the hands of officials who are dishonest. Would you be willing to go and study the refugee situation to help us determine the best way to channel relief directly to the refugees themselves?"

Shortly after the invasion, in the winter of 1980, Gordon-Conwell kindly allowed me to take a leave and go with my wife.

Betty and I, along with Cleo Shook and Mark and Winnie Ritchie (who had been with us in Afghanistan), made a survey of the Afghan refugees along the Afghanistan-Pakistan border, and came across shockingly tragic situations. A Christian nurse from England, Rosemary Weston, accompanied us. She was working with the the United Nations at the time.

One camp was completely made up of women and children. The Communists had come into the town of Kerala, in Eastern Afghanistan, and told the men and boys that they would give them presents. All they had to do was to show up in the town square at 9:00 a.m. the next day.

When the 1,800 men and boys showed up the next day, they were told to line up for their presents. Then the Communists machine-gunned them all down! After that, both the Russian and Afghan Communists took bulldozers and buried the bodies in mass graves. Some of them were wounded but still alive when they were buried. The women and children fled across the border, and this camp at Bajawur held those who had survived.

Shortly after arriving in Pakistan that winter of 1980, we stayed with Gordon and Grace Magney who had been working in Afghanistan until the

Russian invasion had forced them to flee. Cleo Shook, Gordon, and I drew up plans to re-establish the Christian relief agency SERVE, which we had originally set up in Kabul back in 1972, with the approval of the Afghan government. At that time, we had chosen the name from Mark 10:45, where Christ said that He didn't come to be served but to serve. The initials stood for Serving Emergency Relief and Vocational Enterprises.

When first organized in 1972, SERVE had helped the Afghans at the time of a severe famine in the central highlands. No rain had fallen for two years. One out of every three people died of starvation. Many were even forced to eat their donkeys in order to survive. For a Muslim, to eat such an "unclean" animal was unspeakable! However, with the help of an airplane from Mission Aviation Fellowship, we had flown in food, medicine, and clothing for the people. The head of World Vision at the time, Dr. Stanley Mooneyham, from Monrovia, California, had also flown to Afghanistan to provide aid as well.

Now, nearly a decade later, SERVE was once again helping the Afghans. Only this time they were refugees in Pakistan, and we needed the approval of the Pakistani Government, which we finally received. Now we had a recognized Christian relief agency that could be trusted. And it also had the privilege of importing cars and materials free from high import duties. As a result, SERVE was able to pour all its relief funds directly into helping the refugees.

For ten long years, the Afghan freedom fighters hung in there, fighting Communism to the death. Then on February 15, 1989 Russia finally withdrew her armies.

This was a direct answer to prayer. I have always believed that two great heresies of Christianity—Communism and Islam—were clashing in Afghanistan. And so since the invasion of Afghanistan, I had prayed daily, "Lord, whenever You have accomplished Your purposes in Afghanistan, and no longer need Russia there, then force her to withdraw. And may both Russia and Afghanistan be evangelized."

On my car, I had a bumper sticker that read, "Russia out of Afghanistan!"

This amused some of my students who would tell me, "Russia never withdraws from any country."

"Nothing is impossible with God," I would answer.

And the Lord answered my prayer. Russia did withdraw. I really believe that the Soviet withdrawal from Afghanistan set the stage for the total collapse of Communism. Other Soviet-oppressed nations were emboldened to rise up and fight for their own freedom. Communism had begun to crumble.

Now I'm praying that Islam, the other false absolute, will fall, and that millions of Muslims will come to know Jesus Christ as their personal Lord and Savior.

Afghan Freedom Fighters

"What chance is there that the Soviets might be forced to withdraw from Afghanistan?" I asked the military chargé at the American Embassy in Islamabad that winter of 1980, while my wife and I were in the capital of Pakistan. The chargé was a Christian.

"Absolutely no chance whatsoever," he said. That was the American policy, and they were sure that Russia would not pull out.

But everyone underestimated the grit and determination of the Afghan freedom fighters.

Since I had spent twenty-two years in Afghanistan, I knew the people. And I knew the history of their country.

In 1842 the British, who already occupied India and Pakistan, had also invaded Afghanistan. One winter, they decided to move their troops to a warmer climate, going from Kabul, which was cold and mountainous, to Jalalabad, which was subtropical in climate. This was a distance of only 100 miles.

But as the British troops moved from Kabul to Jalalabad, the Afghans wiped out the entire regiment of 16,500 men—slaughtering or capturing them all—except for one man. The sole survivor to reach Jalalabad was the medical officer of the regiment, Dr. Brydon, who lived to tell of the massacre.

From this, I knew that the Russians had not reckoned with the Afghans. If they had read their history, they would not have been so quick to invade Afghanistan.

The Afghans had determined that they would resist the Soviets to the last man. They fought with their hands and with old muzzleloaders. At night they would tunnel under the highways over which the Soviet tanks would be traveling. Later when the heavy armored vehicles would roll over those roads, they would plunge through into the pits below. As the Russian soldiers would scramble out of their tanks, the Afghans would shoot them.

They captured tanks the way you would capture an elephant!

When we were in Pakistan, we talked with Afghan freedom fighters. They told us how they created their own hand grenades. They took old bottles, filled them with gasoline, lit a wick, and then tossed the bottle onto the rear of the tanks. The bottles would explode, with smoke and flames searing the inside of the tanks. As the Russians tried to escape, the Afghans shot them to death.

The men who threw these explosives knew they would probably be killed, as many of them were. Yet they did it anyway. The Russians were stymied.

One Afghan general called Massoud was in the area north of Kabul. He defeated the Russian army eight times! This is the strategy he used.

He built a scale model of the area they were going to attack, showing every tree, house, hill, and mud fort. Then he gave each of his men very precise instructions on what to do and when. On the day of their attack, the Afghans would strike at 4:00 a.m. while the Russians were still asleep. He defeated the Soviets eight times this way!

The first time, the Russians planned to enter the Panjshir Valley through a very narrow pass. Massoud knew of their plans because he had Afghan spies in the Soviet Army. So a couple of weeks before the Russians planned to make this march, Massoud attacked their camp, destroying their MIG fighter planes. This delayed the Soviet's plans by several months.

Finally the Russians mounted their attack.

But Massoud had already laid mines in cliffs at the entrance to the valley. When the Russians began coming through, the mines exploded. Falling rock from the mountain cliffs not only trapped them but completely barricaded their path. Then he wiped them out from the mountains above.

Another thing Massoud did showed his ingenuity. The Russians laid mine fields in the areas around their fortifications. Massoud had his men drive goats before them as mine sweepers. The goats triggered the mines! The Afghans moved right through—and then ate the goats!

Massoud is a genius as a military commander.

The Russians did everything to force the Afghans to surrender. They dropped toys loaded with explosives that blew off children's arms when they picked them up. They shot the animals from helicopters. They set the crops on fire, hoping to starve the people.

The Afghans just kept on fighting!

Finally the United States sent Afghanistan Stinger missiles to destroy Russian aircraft. In one year, Russia lost 273 planes, some of which were filled with troops!

Finally the Soviets gave up and withdrew from Afghanistan by February 15, 1989.

The American planes that transported Stinger missiles to Afghanistan returned to the United States with wounded freedom fighters. Russian bombs had destroyed all the hospitals in the outlying areas.

My wife and I had a wonderful time visiting with some of the Afghans in American hospitals. We even brought a few of them to our home in Gloucester, Massachusetts.

Four who visited with us one weekend had never seen the ocean before, since Afghanistan is completely landlocked. Even on the flight coming here, no one knew their language to tell them to look out the window and see the Atlantic Ocean. They just sat in the plane drinking tea and talking.

When they arrived in the States, they immediately boarded vans for the drive to New Hampshire.

As a result, when they came to our home in Gloucester, which was right on the ocean, they kept staring at the huge expanse of water in utter amazement.

"Does the ocean go up in the spring and down in the fall?" they asked. That's what the lakes and rivers do in Afghanistan because of the melting snow.

"No," I said, "the ocean doesn't go up in the spring and down in the fall, but it does go up and down twice every twenty-four hours because of the moon."

"Because of the moon?!" they exclaimed. They had never heard of the tide before, and this sounded like a tall tale.

I remember one soldier. He showed us his seventeen scars caused by bullets and shrapnel. When he came to the States, he couldn't even walk. He had to use crutches. But he told us that as soon as he could walk, he was going to go back and fight!

After meeting this soldier and hearing him talk, one of my seminary students said, "If we Christians only had the dedication for our Lord that these Afghan freedom fighters have for their nation, we could complete Christ's Commission very quickly!"

Communism began to crumble in Afghanistan because of the courage of the people. They were not afraid to die. They vowed that the Russians were not going to stay in their country and they fought them with whatever they had.

We Don't Have To Tell Everything

Shortly after my wife and I were forced to leave Afghanistan by order of the Muslim government, I was invited to speak about my experiences at the 1974 Lausanne Congress. My topic was on witnessing under political oppression.

We met in small groups to draft the Lausanne Covenant. Paragraph thirteen of the Covenant, to which we were asked to contribute, deals with witnessing under persecution.

Corrie ten Boom was also at the Congress. She had heard of the destruction of the church building in Kabul, Afghanistan, the year before *(see Chapter 8, "Afghanistan's Apostle Paul")*. She said to me, "Krrristee, don't be concerned. There is no panic in heaven!"

Corrie ten Boom also raised an interesting question: Is it permissible to tell a lie to save someone's life? She said that during World War II, when she was hiding Jews in her home in Nazi-occupied Holland, the Gestapo arrived one day.

"Are there any Jews in your home?" they asked.

"No, there are none here," she replied. She felt it was better to lie and save their lives rather than tell the truth and see them shipped off to concentration camps and certain death.

On the other hand, her sister Betsie experienced a similar situation but told the truth. One evening, just as everyone was sitting down to dinner, there was a loud knocking at the door. As Betsie went to answer it, all the Jews quickly crawled under the table to hide behind the tablecloth which reached to the floor.

It was the Gestapo, and they proceeded to search the house.

"Are you hiding any Jews?" they demanded.

"Yes, they are under the table," she answered. The Gestapo were so sure she was lying and making fun of them that they didn't even lift up the tablecloth to see. Instead, they marched right out!

The question was: who was right? Corrie ten Boom for lying to save lives, or her sister Betsie for telling everything to the enemy?

At that meeting in Lausanne, we had a Russian Baptist pastor by the name of the Rev. Ham, who had been sent to prison in the Soviet Union for his faith and given the third degree.

He said that both Corrie and her sister Betsie were wrong.

"It is never right to tell a lie," he said. "Jesus never told a lie. And the Bible says we are not to bear false witness. On the other hand, Betsie was wrong too. Sometimes it is a sin to tell everything. Let me give you an example," he said.

"In Russia, I was in prison and tortured brutally. They tried to force me to reveal the location of a Christian printing press that was publishing portions of Scripture and hymn books. Even if they threatened to kill me, I would never reveal its whereabouts to them, although I knew exactly where it was.

"If I had told the Communists where the printing press was, I would have endangered the lives of many Christians and stopped the work of God.

"What would you have said if the Gestapo had asked you what they asked Corrie ten Boom or Betsie?" someone questioned.

"I would have asked them to look around for themselves. You don't have to lie—neither do you have to tell everything," he said.

From Tea Shop to National Leadership: Charles Soong and the Soong Dynasty

Charles Soong was a little boy in China, during the late 1800's, when his family sent him to the United States to work in his uncle's tea shop in Boston's Chinatown.

He told his uncle that he wanted to get an education.

"No," his uncle protested. "You don't need an education. You're a good worker. Stay in my tea shop."

Since his uncle wouldn't let him go to school, Charles ran away to sea.

He managed to stow away on a ship anchored in Boston harbor. After the ship had put out to sea, he came out to look for food and was discovered by the crew.

The captain of the ship, a Christian, gave Charles a job as cabin boy. The ship sailed down the East coast of America, and Charles ended up in a Methodist revival meeting in the South, where he accepted Christ. With the support of many Christians, Charles was able to realize his lifelong dream of getting an education. Eventually he graduated from seminary and became a pastor.

When he finally returned to China in the late 1880's, it's amazing what God did through him there.

Charles went to Shanghai and headed up the Bible Society. He was a very good businessman as well as a pastor. Later he married a Christian, and he and his wife raised three daughters and one son.

The oldest daughter married a man who later became China's Minister of Finance. His second daughter married Sun Yat-sen, who was the first President of China. This Madame Soong later became Vice-President of the Communist government! The third daughter became Madame Chiang Kai-shek, marrying the Generalissimo. But she would not agree to marry him until he became a Christian! The fourth child, T. V. Soong, his only son, became both Prime Minister and Foreign Minister of China under Chiang Kai-shek.

In 1980, shortly before Madame Soong died, she was visited by Ruth Graham and her sisters Rosa and Virginia, and their brother Clayton Bell. Madame Soong told them at that time that she had never become a Communist.

It's amazing to see the powerful Christian influence wielded by the children of the little boy who ran away from his uncle's tea shop in Boston and came to Christ. The revival we now see going on in China, as millions are coming to Christ, can be traced in some measure to Charles Soong and the influence of his descendants.

Billy Graham and Prevailing Prayer

In 1950 Billy Graham held a crusade in Boston. At that time, only one church in all New England would sponsor him. That was the Park Street Church in Boston, where the senior pastor was Dr. Harold John Ockenga. He invited Billy Graham to speak in his church.

And that's when a revival started. The church could not accommodate the overflow crowds so they had to move into the largest arena in the city, the Boston Garden, where the Celtics play. And even that was filled!

Thousands of people came to Christ.

Dr. Ockenga said that during that time, he and Billy Graham would meet for prayer in his office at the church. They would kneel before the Lord and pray that God would do this not only in Boston, but also in capital cities around the world, especially in the Communist countries—and even in Moscow!

In 1977 Billy Graham was invited to the first preaching tour in Communist Hungary. At the time of this historic occasion in Hungary, Dr. Ockenga was leading a chapel at Gordon-Conwell and recalled their earlier prayers back in 1950.

"Twenty-seven years ago," he said, "Billy and I knelt in prayer asking God to open the Communist countries to Christian crusades. I have prayed that same prayer every day ever since then. And God has now begun to answer."

This was the beginning of many visits which Billy Graham made to Communist countries, including the Soviet Union, where he ministered. When he went to Moscow, the American media said that the Russians would make him a dupe of Communism.

Now, however, some of the leading commentators like Dan Rather acknowledge that Billy Graham had much to do with the collapse of Communism. His visit to North Korea in early April 1992 is an example of God accomplishing the impossible.

Billy Graham's prayers, along with those of Dr. Ockenga and others, have helped bring about the fall of Communism. Behind every news announcement broadcast on television, there is a great spiritual battle being waged continually. Only when we get to heaven will we learn the real story behind world events. Then we will see the powerful influence that prayer has had on the course of history.

Chapter 5

Today's Apostles

The Real John Birch

The real John Birch had nothing at all to do with the Society that bears his name. Rather, he was an evangelical missionary in the interior of China, born of missionary parents who served in India.

When his father, an agricultural expert, developed a severe case of malaria which doctors couldn't cure, he was told to return to the United States. So he came back and bought a farm in Georgia, where young John went to college.

Later John went to China, where he studied Mandarin in Shanghai and was the top student in the language school.

When war broke out between the United States and Japan, John disguised himself as a Chinese coolie. In this way, he traveled back and forth across the Japanese lines ... as an evangelist! He would preach to the Chinese on both sides of the line.

Although the Japanese later tried to capture him, they never succeeded.

Once when John was eating at an inn (he had never married), a Chinese man came up to him and whispered: "I have very important information to share with you in private. Come with me."

When they got outside, the man said, "We have found some Americans!" They had found Jimmy Doolittle's men!

After the Japanese attack on Pearl Harbor, the United States catapulted bombers over Japan, led by Colonel Jimmy Doolittle. After the pilots dropped their bombs over Japan, they flew over China where they bailed out, parachuted to earth, and allowed the planes to crash.

This strategy worked. It took the Japanese by surprise.

When John Birch heard that the Chinese had found Jimmy Doolittle's men, he went to work. He rescued 82 American pilots and helped them escape from China by way of the Burma Road.

The grateful American airmen praised John Birch to General Claire Chennault in charge of the flying Tigers. And Jimmy Doolittle told the General, "You must get hold of that man. He's worth his weight in gold! He could greatly help the war effort."

John Birch was offered a commission in the U.S. Air Force, which he turned down. "But," he said, "if you could make me a chaplain ... "

"I don't have any positions for chaplains," replied the General. "But if you become a regular officer, I'll give you permission to preach as much as you want in any place that you want."

John Birch accepted the offer. And during the remainder of the war, he helped the Americans greatly.

For example, he smuggled radio equipment across Japanese lines in a "honey wagon" he bought from a farmer. (A honey wagon is a euphemism for the carts the Chinese use to transport human fertilizer.) He put all the radio equipment in this wagon, disguised himself as a coolie once again, and went through the Japanese lines.

As he approached the Japanese, the soldiers would grab their noses and shout, "Go through quickly! Go through quickly!"

In this way, he traveled all along the coast of China, meeting with Chinese Christian friends whom he had hired to be "spotters." Whenever they spotted Japanese ships, they would immediately radio the flying Tigers in code—a different code for each day of the week—giving the exact location for each ship.

Whenever Japanese aircraft shot down an American plane, John Birch would be dropped by parachute into that area to rescue the pilot. Disguised as a Chinese national, he would ask where the airmen were. Then he would find them and arrange their rescue.

One time, in central China, the Japanese completely surrounded Chinese forces numbering more than one million soldiers, cutting them off from any help. John Birch parachuted into their midst. He talked the Chinese Army into building an airport right there in the valley where they were. With one million men wielding shovels, the Chinese were able to construct this airport by hand! As soon as it was completed, the Americans flew cargo planes in with all the necessary supplies.

Missionaries were also forced into that valley by the Japanese. When John radioed for a plane to fly them out, he was told, "We're not here to give free rides to missionaries. Haven't you heard there's a war on!"

"Tell General Chennault that I have a bag full of classified information for him. Have him send a plane over," John Birch replied.

The plane arrived. And John loaded the bag of military secrets on the plane, and then filled the plane with missionaries! That's the way he evacuated many missionaries from Central China.

The airport built by hand not only helped supply the Chinese army but it also served as a landing field for American aircraft on their way to bomb Japan.

During the war, John Birch saw what the Communists were up to, and they realized it. Two weeks after the war ended, the Communists captured John Birch along with a Chinese officer, also a Christian.

The Communists forced John to kneel, then tied his hands behind his back, and bayoneted him. After killing him, they slashed his face, completely disfiguring him, so no one would recognize him. Then they tossed him into a ditch. They also bayoneted the Chinese officer and threw him into the ditch, leaving him for dead. But that night, several Chinese passing by heard the officer moaning. They took him to a hospital, where he lived to tell what had happened to John Birch.

When word reached Washington of John Birch's death, some U.S. senators who favored the Chinese Communist leader Mao Tse-tung tried to cover up the truth. They claimed that Mao was not a real Communist, only an agrarian reformer. They didn't want it leaked out that an American officer had been killed by the Communists.

As a result, John Birch's parents received a letter from the Pentagon stating that their son had been killed in China by a stray bullet.

After they received the telegram, a soldier came to their home to ask if they had heard any more details concerning their son.

"No, nothing more than this telegram," they told him.

The soldier then asked if he could see the telegram. Mrs. Birch went to get it. While the soldier was reading the telegram, he set his clipboard down on the table. On top was an official memo which stated, "John Birch was killed by Chinese Communists."

"What's this?" Mrs. Birch cried out when she saw the memo.

"Oh, you weren't supposed to see that," the officer blurted. "That was classified information."

"You mean I'm not supposed to know what happened to my own son?" This tipped her off to the attempted cover-up.

So Mrs. Birch went to Washington and persuaded Senator William Knowland, of California, to investigate the matter. It was revealed that John Birch had indeed been killed by the Chinese Communists.

Finally, with the Freedom of Information Act, the Government's classified documents on him were released. James and Marti Hefley include these in their book, *The Secret File on John Birch* (Wheaton, Ill.: Tyndale House, 1980).

Only after this, was the John Birch Society formed. He personally had nothing to do with it. They adopted his name because they were strong anti-Communists. And John Birch, an American missionary and officer, had been killed by the Communists.

I think the story of the *real* John Birch would make a thrilling movie—equal to the award-winning film *Chariots of Fire*, about Eric Liddell, another missionary to China.

"I Want A God Who Answers Prayer"

Irene Webster-Smith, an Irish missionary, worked in Japan among Shinto believers before the Second World War. When the war ended, General Douglas MacArthur invited her to return to Japan because he had heard that she was a wonderful missionary and the Japanese Christians respected her greatly.

She returned to Tokyo and worked with students there through the Japanese branch of InterVarsity. Before long, they had outgrown their quarters and needed a center urgently. Irene found a house for sale right in the heart of the student population. But when she inquired of the owner, a woman, she was disappointed.

"I'm sorry, it has just been sold," the woman said.

"If the agreement falls through," Irene said, "here is my telephone number."

"Oh, it won't fall through. We all agreed."

But the next day, the owner telephoned her.

"I don't know what happened but the interested buyer has backed out," she said, and asked Irene to come and talk with her.

Her selling price was the equivalent of $18,000 for the house and property.

"Do you have the money?" she asked.

"No, I don't," replied Irene. "But I believe in God and He owns the universe so He has the $18,000. But would you let me pay that sum in installments, giving you the equivalent of $3,000 for the next six months, due at the end of each month?" The owner agreed.

Since Irene didn't have any money, she immediately went to prayer. Her life verse was Philippians 4:6, "Do not be anxious about anything, but in *everything by prayer* and petition, with thanksgiving, present your requests to God." And at the end of each month, the money would come in!

The owner of the house had given Irene an account number at the bank where she was to deposit the money at the end of each month. One month Irene did not have the $3,000 on the Friday it was due.

But it just so happened that the bank called her that day.

"We're taking inventory so would you please wait until Monday to make your deposit," they asked.

Now, during that weekend, Irene had been invited to speak before some of the American troops stationed in Japan. After she spoke, they took up an offering for her mission and, by the next day, she had her $3,000!

Finally, when she had paid off the entire $18,000, the woman selling the house, who was a Shintoist, invited her for a visit.

"You know," said the woman, "I have offered thousands and thousands of prayers at the Shinto shrine, but none of them have ever been answered. I had two sons and a husband, and all three were killed in the Second World War. I prayed to the Shinto gods to protect them, but my prayers weren't answered. So now I am alone. I don't need this house anymore. That's why I'm selling it.

"When you told me that your God would hear your prayers and answer them, I decided in my heart that if He did it, I would ask Him to be my God. I want to have a God who answers prayer."

So Irene Webster-Smith led this Japanese woman to Christ.

I went to visit Irene there in Tokyo on two different occasions. That property is now the headquarters for much of the Christian outreach in Japan and is worth millions of dollars. It features a high-rise building that houses a large Christian bookstore, the Christian Literature Crusade office, radio stations, and Bible schools. It has been the headquarters for InterVarsity and World Vision as well as many other Christian organizations.

All this because of Irene Webster-Smith's prayer!

Faith That Moves Mountains

Irene Webster-Smith also started an orphanage for Japanese girls, and led them all to Christ.

One evening during their devotions, they read Mark 11:22-24, where Jesus said: "Have faith in God ... I tell you the truth, if anyone says to this mountain, 'Go, throw yourself into the sea,' and does not doubt in his heart but believes that what he says will happen, it will be done for him.

Therefore, I tell you, whatever you ask for in prayer, believe that you have received it, and it will be yours."

One little girl asked, "*Sensei* (Teacher), did Jesus really mean what He said?"

Irene Webster-Smith answered, "Of course, He meant what He said. Why do you ask?"

The child went on to say, "There is a large mountain between our Sunrise Orphanage and the Sea of Japan. If this were removed and cast into the sea, we would have a beautiful view of the ocean."

This was too much for Irene Webster-Smith's faith. She tried to soften the blow of disappointment by telling the little girl that Jesus did not necessarily mean a physical mountain, but rather that if we had problems in our lives and asked Him to remove them, He could. However, the child added, "But, Sensei, Jesus said that if you say to *this mountain*. He was talking about a real one. I'm going to ask Him to take it away."

Not long after, they noticed that there were bulldozers on the top of that mountain. When Irene asked the workers what they were doing, they told her that the Japanese Government had decided to use it for fill. So they were going to transport it all and throw it into the shallow part of the sea, in order to reclaim land.

The little girl's prayer was literally answered! And the Sunrise Orphanage had a beautiful view of the Sea of Japan.

Moody's Key to Revival: A Clean Slate

God used Dwight L. Moody in a mighty way because he obeyed His Word.

Once when Moody was preaching, he saw a man in the audience with whom he had had a disagreement. Immediately he stopped preaching and announced, "Let's sing hymn Number 56."

Then while everyone was standing up and singing the hymn, Mr. Moody stepped down from the pulpit and went up to that man. Putting his arm around him, Moody said, "Will you forgive me? I'm sorry that I had that disagreement with you."

The man forgave him.

Then Dwight L. Moody returned to the pulpit, had everyone sit down, and began preaching with new power, all because he took God's Word seriously!

In Matthew 5, Jesus said, "If you remember your brother has something against you, go and make it right before you offer your gift to God."

In Matthew 18, He says, "If you have something against someone else, you should go and try to make it right. If he won't hear you, then take two or three. If that person still won't hear you, then take it to the whole church." Christ has given us a wonderful way to overcome conflicts between believers. This is the Number One problem that many Christians face.

The Moravians had this same problem at Herrnhut. They had many personality conflicts even though they were Christians and refugees as well.

Finally, after much prayer and repentance, and after they had made things right with each other, a great revival broke out in 1727. God worked in a mighty way.

Charles Finney's definition of a spiritual awakening was "regaining your first love for Christ." That's what our Lord said to the church in Ephesus: "Your works are wonderful but I have one thing against you, it is that you have lost your first love." When the Moravians regained their first love for Christ and each other, they experienced revival, and this led to their reaching out to the world through missions.

Pacific Islanders Lead Downed Pilot to Christ

During the Second World War, many of the Allied troops owed their lives to the sacrifices made by the early missionaries, especially in the South Sea Islands. The people there had once been cannibals but were now Christians.

I knew one New Zealand pilot who was shot down over the Pacific by the Japanese. He parachuted to safety onto one of the South Sea Islands. Two of the local people, who happened to be Christians, found him and led him to safety. One man led the way while the pilot followed. Suddenly the New Zealander noticed the other South Sea Islander trailing behind him.

"What is he doing?" asked the pilot in Pidgin English.

"Oh, he is covering your tracks." The second man, with his big bare feet, was carefully concealing the pilot's footprints so that the Japanese would not be able to track him down.

The local Islanders not only took care of this pilot but they also witnessed to him about Christ! Today he is a minister of the Gospel—because South Sea Islanders told him about Jesus!

A Monument in Gratitude for God's Word

At the top of a hill in the city of Macao, far from the gambling casinos below, stands an old Anglican church and cemetery. Two memorials capture the eye.

One is the gravestone of Robert Morrison, a missionary to China who translated the entire Bible into the language of the people. The other is a monument which the Chinese Christians built to thank God for sending them Robert Morrison!

Robert Morrison volunteered to go to China in 1807 to learn the language and translate the Scriptures. However, the British East India Company, which controlled the China trade, did not want a missionary there. So he sailed from England, around North and South America, and then to China. The trip took him seven months.

When he reached China, however, he faced a legal obstacle. It was against the law then to teach the language to any foreigner. So Robert Morrison had to learn the language in secret.

In 1982 Betty and I went to Macao to visit the grave of this courageous man, who would not let anything stop him from accomplishing the task that God had called him to do.

David Livingstone in Africa

David Livingstone was one of the greatest missionaries who ever lived. A native of Scotland, he went to Southern Africa to visit Robert Moffat, who was a pioneer worker there and from whom he learned a great deal. There, Livingstone fell in love with the Moffats' daughter, Mary, and they were married.

Robert Moffat made a very interesting observation:

"We have all eternity in which to celebrate our victories but only one short life before sunset in which to win them."

As that little couplet goes:

> *One life to live, it will soon be past;*
> *Only what's done for Christ will last.*

When it comes to missions, I think this is so important. We only have one life—unlike the Hindu philosophy that we go through many lives. And God wants us to invest it for Him.

God has given us talents, life, and His clear will and purpose for our lives—yet what a tragedy it is that so many waste and bury their talents instead of investing them.

David Livingstone invested his talents for God. Not only was he a medical doctor but he was also an explorer. His great vision was to reach the interior of Africa, which no white man had set foot in at that time. He said that he was willing to go anywhere provided it was forward. He once observed that God had only one Son, and He became a foreign missionary.

One time he said that he could see the smoke of a thousand villages—none of which had ever heard of the name of the Lord Jesus Christ.

David Livingstone had a great passion to make the entire Christian world aware of what was going on in Africa. He worked hard to expose the human tragedy of slavery. For this, the slave traders tried to kill him. Yet he was able to say: "In Christ's work, we are immortal until God's time comes for us to die." He was undaunted and continued with his work.

One night when enemies had surrounded him and certain death was imminent, he wrote down his exact location from a reading of the stars—in order to keep the record of his explorations—and then opened his Bible to Psalm 37: "Commit your way to the Lord, trust also in Him and He will bring it to pass."

He didn't know whether he would live through the night or not, but he committed himself to God and went to sleep. In the morning, his enemies had vanished!

Another time he was attacked by a lion, which knocked him unconscious and broke his shoulder. The Africans saved his life.

All this time, the world didn't know if David Livingstone were dead or alive. A correspondent from Chicago, by the name of Stanley, went into deepest Africa to look for Livingstone. When he found him, he used that famous expression: "Dr. Livingstone, I presume?" Stanley came to Christ through David Livingstone's testimony.

Stanley's encounter with Livingstone completely transformed his life. When Stanley came back, he wrote about his adventures, and this was the beginning of a mission he started for Africa.

One night David Livingstone was kneeling in prayer in his tent with his Bible open before him. The next morning his African friends found him dead—yet still on his knees when he went to be with His Lord.

The Africans were so grateful for all that he had done for them that they said his heart belonged in Africa. So they cut out his heart and buried it there. Then they carried his body over 4,000 miles across Africa, through the jungles, to the ocean.

The British Government sent a warship to transport the body back for burial in London's Westminster Abbey, since Livingstone had also served as a "tentmaker" or British consul. But before they buried him, the Government wanted to be sure it was Livingstone's body, so they examined it for evidence of a broken shoulder! Sure enough, they found it, and they buried him in Westminster Abbey.

The Beloved Amy Carmichael of India

Although Amy Carmichael was a missionary who lived and worked in southern India most of her life, she did not set out with this purpose. She had originally intended to serve in Japan.

While serving in Japan, however, her health failed and she was forced to return to England. During the trip to England, the ship stopped in southern India, where she found the weather was better for her health. And there she returned to spend the rest of her life as a missionary.

Amy started an orphanage to save the little Indian girls who were being forced to serve as temple prostitutes in the Hindu temples—as well as little boys who were being used for homosexual purposes in the same way. Through much prayer and sacrifice, she was able to save hundreds of these little girls and boys from this tragic life. Even today there are many doctors and Christian leaders in India who owe their lives to Amy Carmichael.

In addition to having a great ministry in southern India, Amy was an outstanding writer and poet. This is one of her poems:

> *Captain Beloved, battle wounds were Thine.*
> *Let me not wonder if some hurt be mine.*
> *But rather, let this my wonder be,*
> *That I should share a battle wound with Thee.*

The Little Girl Who Started World Vision

When Dr. Bob Pierce was in China, preaching the Gospel for Youth For Christ, he found a little girl starving by the roadside. Taking her to a Christian orphanage, he asked the lady in charge if she would take care of the girl. The lady said she could not.

"Why not?" Dr. Pierce asked.

"I have already cut down my own food portions to one fourth the usual," she answered. "I'm feeding three other orphans with the remainder. We just don't have enough food for another child."

"Would money help?" he asked.

"Oh yes," she replied.

"How much would it cost to take care of this little girl—her food, clothing, medical care, and everything?"

The lady said it would take the equivalent of $5 a month. So he gave her a check for $120, and the lady took the little girl in.

When Bob returned to the United States and told this story, others wanted to sponsor an orphan too. He had to form an organization to officially handle the contributions.

That's how he started World Vision. All because of that one little orphan girl! And today World Vision is taking care of more than one million children around the world.

George Whitefield in New England

During the first Great Awakening in America, George Whitefield preached in New England and received a great response. When he came to Boston for the first time in 1740, a liberal minister approached him.

"I'm sorry you've come to Boston," the clergyman said.

"The devil is sorry too," was Whitefield's reply.

People were so eager to hear him in Boston that they overflowed into the aisles of the church where he was to speak, making it impossible for Whitefield to even enter the building to preach! So one man placed a ladder at the window and Whitefield climbed up, crawled in through the window, and then got into the pulpit.

As Whitefield preached, the Holy Spirit convicted the people in a mighty demonstration of power. Some jumped out the balcony and windows. Four people were killed in that first meeting.

As word of Whitefield's preaching spread, no building was large enough to contain the crowds that came to hear him. The gatherings were then moved outside to the Boston Common, where crowds exceeded 20,000!

Although they had no public address system in those days, Whitefield had a powerful voice that could be heard at great distances, even in the open air. He had been trained to project his voice as an actor does. Benjamin Franklin, who was a scientist, was so intrigued by Whitefield's voice that he conducted an experiment in Philadelphia. He went thirteen city blocks away from where Whitefield was preaching—and could still hear him!

George Whitefield also preached on Squam Rock in Gloucester and in Ipswich, Massachusetts. The church in Ipswich was supposed to be haunted. Yet he preached with such power they say the devil jumped right out of the steeple!

Whitefield exorcised Satan from that church. Even today the people of Ipswich will show you a rock bearing the devil's footprint, as he fled from George Whitefield's preaching. Although this story of the footprint is apocryphal, it is a tradition which shows that people recognized the power of God in him.

Whitefield also preached in the woods at Pulpit Rock in Rowley, where 2,000 farmers stopped work and gathered to hear him. Finally he preached at Newburyport. There the people were so eager to hear him that a large crowd gathered at the doorstep of the pastor's manse, where Whitefield was staying and, after supper, pleaded with him to preach. Whitefield held a candle in a holder. Then he preached until the candle went out. After that he went upstairs to bed.

That night he died.

He is buried under the pulpit of Old South Presbyterian Church in Newburyport, Massachusetts.

The Great Commission Was His Visa

Before Iraq forced out all the Christian missionaries in 1967, Dr. John Van Ness was a missionary there with the Dutch Reformed Church. He worked in southern Iraq in the city of Busra until he felt God calling him to the coast of Saudi Arabia in the Persian Gulf. So he applied for a visa but the Saudi government sent word back that no missionaries were allowed. Despite this, he still felt that's where the Lord wanted him to go. So although he had no visa, he boarded a ship for Saudi Arabia.

"Where is your visa?" the officials demanded when he arrived.

Dr. Van Ness took his Arabic Bible and turned to Mark 15:15-16.

"These are the words of the Prophet Jesus," he said. "Go into all the world and preach the Gospel to every creature, and those who believe and are baptized will be saved, but those who do not believe will be condemned."

"Is this part of the world?" he asked.

"Oh, yes," they replied.

"All right, this is not only my permission," he said, "but it is my commission! I'm ordered to come to tell you this good news about Jesus Christ. Do you have any tea?"

"Oh, yes, sit down, sit down." Then they served him tea, accepting the Bible as his visa! He then shared the good news of Jesus Christ with them.

Strange Birds Open Up Nepal

Nepal first opened its doors to the Gospel because of a missionary's love of exotic birds.

Friends of ours, Dr. and Mrs. Robert Fleming, were missionaries in India. Mrs. Bertha Fleming was a medical doctor, and her husband was a teacher in a Christian school there.

Dr. Robert Fleming's hobby was ornithology since he loved the study of birds.

It happened that one of the princes from the royal family of Nepal came to India to study, attending the school where Dr. Fleming taught.

When he realized Dr. Fleming's deep interest in birds, the prince invited him to visit Nepal. "We have many beautiful birds in Nepal," said the prince. "Why don't you come and study them?"

"I'm not allowed to go into Nepal," Dr. Fleming said. "No missionaries are allowed."

"Look," said the prince. "I'll invite you! Come as my guest!"

So he did.

But Mrs. Fleming would not allow her husband to go without a medical doctor, in case he got sick there. She asked a missionary doctor from Scandinavia to accompany her husband.

The two men went to Nepal in the summer and discovered birds no one knew existed. Dr. Fleming had a wonderful time studying them. And his companion was kept busy as well. As soon as the people of Nepal discovered the Scandinavian missionary was a medical doctor, they flocked to him by the hundreds.

When it came time for the two men to leave Nepal, the people pleaded, "Don't go, we need you."

"If you get permission for us, we'll be back," they promised.

That's how missionaries were first allowed to enter Nepal in 1953. Ten missions had workers on the borders of that country, praying and waiting to go in. They all went in together under the United Mission to Nepal.

Forty years ago there were hardly any Christians in Nepal. Today there are tens of thousands!

Nepal had a law that anyone who baptized a person would be sentenced to five years in prison. Then the pastors who were jailed led many of their fellow prisoners to Christ! The more the government has tried to stop Christianity, the more it has grown. And recently they have been granted a greater measure of freedom.

Revival Among the Zulus

When my wife and I were visiting in South Africa, we went to the site of the Kwa-Sizabantu revival which began in the late 1960's. The Lord used a missionary from Germany—Erlo Stegen—as His instrument to bring about that revival in Zululand.

In 1967, Erlo Stegen was in deep despair. His work among the Zulus had brought nothing but problems and failures. He felt that Satan was attacking him because he knew this region was a center for witchcraft and the occult found in African traditional religions.

"Lord," he prayed, "You have promised we would not only do the works You did but even greater works. Where are they?"

God spoke to him through 1 Peter 5: 5-6: "God resists the proud but gives grace to the humble. Humble yourselves therefore under the mighty hand of God, that in due time, He may exalt you."

Erlo suddenly realized that what had been blocking the flow of God's power was not Satan, but his own pride. He also realized that if God had blessed him, it would have made him prouder.

So he fell down on his face and asked God to forgive him for his pride. The Lord did that.

Almost immediately a revival broke out in that area. And the first to be converted were the witch doctors and witches.

Since then, the revival has continued in an amazing way. People come there every day from all over the world. To handle the crowds, they are building an auditorium that can seat 10,000 people—up there in the mountains of Zululand!

They also have a hospital there but it's for patients who are terminally ill. The Zulus go there to pray for these patients.

And amazing miracles have taken place!

You can read about these miracles in the book by Dr. Kurt Koch, *God Among the Zulus* (published in Natal, RSA, 1951). He writes of a woman who had died but was raised from the dead after the Zulus prayed for her. After she was brought back to life, she told them how she went to heaven and heard such wonderful choirs that she wanted to start a heavenly choir here on earth! And while my wife Betty and I were there along with David Bliss (Gordon-Conwell '79) and his wife Debbie, we heard this beautiful Zulu choir. They sing in English, German, Zulu, Afrikans, and Russian (they beam radio programs to Russia).

It was a thrill to see this revival. I believe this is the answer to the problems in South Africa, namely, people seeking the Lord first, praying for revival, then reaching out together in missions.

Gregory and the First Christian Nation: Armenia

The first Christian nation in the world was Armenia, thanks to Gregory, later called Gregory the Illuminator because he evangelized the whole country for Christ.

Gregory was born in Armenia, then went as an "international student" to the Holy Land, where he found Christ as his Savior. This shows the importance of witnessing to international students who come to the United States. Just look at what God did through this young man!

After returning to Armenia, Gregory was appointed to an important government post by the King, who had been his friend since childhood.

When the King went to worship in the pagan temples, Gregory had to accompany him but he refused to worship the idols. This angered the King greatly.

"If you don't worship the idols, I must have you killed," the King threatened.

"I'm sorry," said Gregory. "But I now believe in Jesus, and the Scriptures say you should worship no one besides the Lord your God."

In a fit of rage, the King had Gregory thrown into a deep well to die. He was imprisoned at the bottom of that well for thirteen years! Thanks to a wonderful lady who supplied him with food each day, he was able to survive. She would tie a basket of food to a rope and drop the rope into the well.

Being in solitary confinement, Gregory spent his time praying for his nation and for individuals. He interceded for the sick who needed healing, as these prayer requests came to him from the lady who brought him his food each day. He would pray from the bottom of the well, and the Lord would heal them! Soon more and more people brought their requests to him.

One day the King became dangerously ill. No doctor could help him.

"Let's try Gregory," one of them said. "His prayers have healed many sick people, why don't we ask him to pray for the King?"

So, after thirteen years, the King ordered Gregory to be released from prison.

"You pray for people and they are healed," the King said.

"God does it," said Gregory. "I don't. But I do ask God."

"I'm very ill, no physician can help me. Will you pray for me?"

Gregory prayed for the King, and the King was healed! The King was so grateful that he commissioned Gregory to go out and evangelize the entire country and bring them to Christ! Gregory even baptized the entire army by immersion! Led by Gregory, the Armenians destroyed all their pagan idols and temples and then built Christian churches on these sites.

Before long, the entire population was converted to Christ in a mass movement, Christianity was adopted as the national religion, and Armenia became the first Christian nation in the world.

David du Plessis: "Mr. Pentecost"

Dr. David du Plessis was called "Mr. Pentecost" because God used him in the great awakening of the Holy Spirit around the world.

On one occasion, when David went to speak at Yale University, a certain professor told his students: "After he speaks, I'm going to ask him questions which will tie him up in knots."

When Dr. du Plessis had finished, the professor stood up and asked a question.

Dr. du Plessis not only answered that question but immediately went on to add:

"Now, it follows that the next logical question would be ..." And he proceeded to take the words right out of the man's mouth. He continued on in this way, answering the professor's questions before he could even ask them!

The professor was struck speechless. He was so dumbfounded that he sat down.

"Why didn't you go on asking questions?" some of his students asked him later.

"I see Dr. du Plessis knows his subject," the professor replied.

Well, the Holy Spirit had given David a word of wisdom as well as a word of knowledge.

I heard David du Plessis speak on another occasion. "So that we'll save time," he told the group, "instead of asking your questions out loud, ask your questions directly of the Lord—in your heart—and the Lord will give me the answer."

He would look right at a person, know exactly what he was thinking, and then answer his question.

That was the work of the Holy Spirit and God was glorified.

A Trial Heard 'Round the World

A Swedish missionary in Pakistan, with the habit of passing out Scripture, found himself a major celebrity overnight when he tried this in Afghanistan.

Carl Nielsen always offered the Scriptures to shopkeepers after purchasing an item. When he visited Afghanistan, he continued to do the same, not realizing how sensitive the Afghan Muslims were.

After making a purchase in Kabul, he gave the man a copy of the Gospel of Luke in Pashtu. Someone had been watching.

"Oh, could I have a copy?" he asked. So Carl Nielsen gave him a copy as well.

Then another Muslim saw this and began shouting, "There's a foreigner here spreading propaganda." Immediately a huge crowd gathered.

The police soon came and asked what was going on. They were told that the Swedish man was distributing literature. Of course, the police arrested him on the spot and took him to his hotel room, where his wife and three children had been waiting for him. They placed him under house arrest.

I went to see Carl Nielsen and his family at the hotel. A policeman sat outside the door the whole time, not allowing them to leave their room. Finally they allowed his wife and children to go and come but they kept him isolated in his hotel room until the matter could be resolved.

After reading the Gospel of Luke, the Afghan officials then pressed charges against him.

First, the government charged that the New Testament was unnecessary. Although the New Testament, according to the Koran, was the Word of God, the Koran had been revealed later and made the New Testament unnecessary. Therefore, the Bible was not allowed in Afghanistan.

Second, the government charged that "this book says that Jesus is the Son of God but the Koran says that Jesus was the son of Mary. Therefore the Koran is right and this is wrong."

The Muslims were concerned when they read in Luke about Christ's baptism, how the Holy Spirit came upon him, and when God spoke from heaven: "This is My Beloved Son, in Whom I am well pleased."

Tragically, not a single portion of either the New or the Old Testaments had been translated into Arabic until well after Mohammed's death, so Mohammed never had a chance to read the Bible in the only language he knew. As a result, there are no quotations from the Bible in the Koran—only stories gleaned from nominal Christians Mohammed had met.

This was a tragic failure of Christians not to have translated the Bible almost 600 years after the death and resurrection of Christ.

Mohammed thought that Christians worshiped a holy family: God the father, Mary the mother, and Jesus the son. Because Mohammed had seen people worship pictures of Mary, the Koran attacks the doctrine that Jesus is the Son of God. The Muslims misunderstand it. Even today, if you talk with a Muslim, this is the major stumbling block. We Christians believe that Jesus is the Son of God, but the Muslims have the idea that the Trinity is a holy family.

It's amazing that of the two charges brought against Carl Nielsen, the first was against the Word of God, and the second against the Son of God!

Since the judge who was to try the case was a Muslim priest, he was prepared to make this a test case for missionaries and give him a stiff sentence. But just before the trial, the judge dropped dead of a heart attack! The Afghans, who are very quick to see omens in events, became afraid.

Then the press entered the scene. An Australian correspondent for United Press International, looking for a good story, went to interview the missionary and his family in their hotel room. He then flew back to Delhi and filed his article, complete with photos. The story appeared in newspapers all around the world! In fact, I even saw it with pictures in the *Philadelphia Bulletin!*

The correspondent could have slanted his story against the missionary, but he didn't. Instead, he treated him very favorably because his own father was a pastor in Australia.

"Can you imagine arresting someone for giving out a portion of the New Testament?" he wrote. He was very sympathetic.

This embarrassed the Afghan government.

Then one of Dr. Harold Ockenga's former assistants, Dr. Dudley Woodberry— who had studied Islamics at Harvard and is now Dean of the School of World Mission at Fuller—came to Afghanistan. I introduced him to the Afghan attorney who had been hired by Sweden to defend the missionary. The lawyer had intended to plead guilty on behalf of his client and then aim for the lowest possible fine. But then Dr. Woodberry showed the Afghan attorney how the New Testament was indeed the Word of God according to the Koran. He knew more about the Koran than the lawyer.

"This is wonderful," the attorney said. "We're not going to plead guilty. We're going to plead innocent!"

They finally found another judge brave enough to try the case. The Afghan lawyer defended the missionary successfully. And all religious charges were dropped.

Carl Nielsen was fined the equivalent of $23 for handing out literature without a special permit from the Ministry of Culture and Information. And then the family was free to return to their missionary work in Pakistan.

Harold Ockenga Redeems the Time While Flying

At the back of every book he read, Dr. Harold Ockenga would carefully jot down the key ideas he had gleaned from the author. His library is filled with these notations, giving him easy access to the riches inside. This collection has been donated to Gordon-Conwell, where you can still read his handwritten notes.

And he read prodigiously.

In the late '40's and '50's, while Dr. Ockenga was pastoring Park Street Church in Boston on Sundays, he was commuting every week to Pasadena, California, where he spent week days serving as President of Fuller Seminary, which he helped found. He did this for eleven years!

To make the most productive use of his time, he made it a point to read at least one book on every flight between Boston and Los Angeles.

The people at Fuller pleaded with him to move to Pasadena. "You're going to kill yourself commuting like this," they said.

But the people at the Park Street Church loved him so much they held four separate days of prayer and fasting, praying that Dr. Ockenga would not leave New England! And he didn't.

Finally, after eleven years at Fuller, Dr. Ockenga returned to New England full-time and became President of both Gordon-Conwell and Gordon College.

Phone Books Help Complete Christ's Commission

Rochunga and Mawii Pudaite are from the state of Nagaland in northeastern India where not too long ago the people were headhunters. In the late 1800's, a Baptist missionary went to Nagaland, and today the majority of the Nagas are evangelical Christians.

Rochunga was in Delhi when he had an attack of appendicitis, but he didn't have enough money for the operation. There he met Dr. Bob Pierce who founded World Vision. Dr. Pierce paid for the operation, a sum equivalent in rupees to $15. And then, impressed that Rochunga was a very intelligent young man, he arranged for him to receive a scholarship to Wheaton College.

While Rochunga was at Wheaton, he translated the entire New Testament into his own tribal language.

Now Rochunga is married to Mawii, also from Nagaland, and together they have come up with the unique idea of Bibles for the World, the name of their organization.

Throughout the world, people who have telephones are among the up-and-coming ones not easily reached by missionaries. Missionaries are generally drawn to the sick, the poor, the hungry, and those in great need.

So Rochunga and Mawii have started this organization to send New Testaments, in the local language, to every telephone listing in the world. And they've done it for a number of countries.

I happened to meet Rochunga and his wife at O'Hare airport in Chicago, where they were on their way to Central America to collect telephone books.

They even sent New Testaments to Moscow before the collapse of Communism, under a reciprocal agreement for literature distribution between India and what was then the Soviet Union. These New Testaments went to all the telephone listings in the Moscow phone book. And to make sure these reached their destination, a Russian-speaking Christian went to Moscow and called telephone numbers at random to see if the New Testaments had arrived.

"Oh yes! We did receive ours. Thank you very much," the answers came.

Having completed that pilot project for Moscow, Rochunga started doing the same for the rest of Russia.

Bibles for the World has also sent New Testaments to every phone listing throughout India. I saw the New Testament that they sent. It has the Taj Mahal on the cover in color, which the Indians love! You open it, and instead of starting with Matthew, it starts with the Gospel of John. Indians like the Gospel of John because they are of a philosophical mindset, a part of their Hindu background.

Even closed countries are no barrier. Rochunga and Mawii have sent New Testaments to Malaysia, where it's against the law to witness to Muslims. Many people told them they were not allowed to do that, but they had already done it. Furthermore, they received many replies from Muslims in Malaysia thanking them for the Bibles. These Malays who had open hearts to receive God's Word recognized that it was "more to be desired than gold."

Victory for Christ in the Comoro Islands

At the Lausanne II Congress in Manila, in July 1989, we heard many inspiring testimonies that stirred us deeply, given by people who had suffered terribly for Christ,

Among them was a man who became the first Muslim in his nation to come to Christ. He lived in the Comoro Islands, off the coast of Africa in the Indian Ocean.

After this man had become a Christian in 1973, he went abroad for three years to study the Bible. As soon as he returned home, he was immediately arrested at the airport by Muslim officials and thrown into prison.

Now his prison cell was no ordinary one. It was about the size of a narrow coffin standing on end. It forced him to stand continuously. There was neither room to sit down nor lie down. For three long months, he stood in his cell this way.

"Lord, how can I sleep?" he prayed. And the Lord enabled him to sleep while standing up!

The prison guards fed him a diet of rice and salt, a mixture which nearly gagged him. However, when he prayed to the Lord for help, the rice and salt not only became tolerable, it tasted delicious!

At the end of three months, this man was brought before a group of Muslim priests to be judged.

"You are a condemned man because you left Islam and became a Christian," the judge told him. "But we'll let you choose your own punishment. First, you can be shot by a firing squad. Second, you can leave this country and never return." This meant he would never again see his wife and eight children.

"Third, you can be sentenced to life imprisonment and return to the same cell, where you will stay until you die.

"Which do you choose?" the judge asked. "To be shot, to leave the country, or to stand in this box until you die?"

The Christian fell to his knees, lifted his face to heaven, and prayed, "Lord Jesus, I don't know which one to choose. You show me and I will obey You."

Now, Muslims never pray that way. Nor had they ever heard anyone talking directly to God. "He's crazy!" they exclaimed. "He's out of his mind! Let him go!"

So they released him. And he went free.

Because they wanted to see what he would do now, the Muslims had a detective spy on him. Well, he led the detective to Christ!

"Now there are 107 Christians in my country," he said.

It was wonderful to hear his testimony. And it shows us how important it is to intercede continually in prayer for Christians who are suffering persecution in other countries.

Attracted to Jesus in the Koran

While Hussein was a student at the University of Kabul in Afghanistan during the 1950's, he made an amazing discovery. The Koran has much to say about Jesus, and Hussein discovered that Jesus was a greater Wonder Worker than Mohammed! The Koran tells how Christ raised the dead, caused the blind to see and the lame to walk. The Koran says that Jesus' prophecies were fulfilled. Even more amazing to Hussein, the Koran says that Jesus was without sin, that He ascended to heaven and is alive there today.

"If Jesus is a greater Wonder Worker than Mohammed, I want to find out more about this Jesus," Hussein thought to himself.

But no matter how hard he tried, he could not find a copy of the Bible in Afghanistan to read for himself.

Finally, Hussein learned that one of his university professors, a Communist, owned a Persian New Testament. When he asked this professor if he could borrow it, the man replied, "No, no, no. It is a very dangerous book. If anyone found out that I had given it to you, I would be in trouble as well as you. No, you cannot borrow it."

Yet Hussein would not give up. He kept after the professor until he wore him down, like the persistent widow who sought help from the judge who didn't fear God, in Luke 18.

Finally the professor relented. "All right, I'll make a pact with you," he said. "I will let you borrow my New Testament for one week, but only under two conditions. First, you must never tell anyone where you got it, no matter what. Second, after you return it, you must never ask me for it again. I don't want you pestering me anymore. Is that understood?"

Hussein agreed to these terms, and the professor loaned him the New Testament.

Back in his dormitory room, Hussein spent all that week reading the New Testament. He literally devoured it. Because he lived in the dormitory with other students, he bought a flashlight so he could read the New Testament even under the bedcovers, after everyone had fallen asleep. He had only one week and he was not going to waste a minute.

Now a Christian professor, Lloyd Halladay, was also teaching at that same university, having come to Afghanistan as a tentmaker. He too had a New Testament in Persian. But when Hussein asked to borrow his copy, the professor hesitated.

"I'm sorry," said Professor Halladay. "I can't loan it to you because there is no religious freedom in Afghanistan." He was afraid that Hussein was not sincere. The police had used such a ploy before. One time before, they had sent a student to spy on a Christian, pretending to seek answers to spiritual questions. Then the government had expelled the Christian from the country.

Yet Professor Halladay never forgot Hussein's request. And when he had completed his teaching contract, and was returning to the States, he took Hussein aside and said, "Remember, you asked me for my New Testament? Well, I'm going back to the States now, and if you want it, you'll find it in the desk drawer in the lecture hall. You can go and get it. It's yours."

Hussein rushed to the lecture hall, flung open the desk drawer, and pulled out the New Testament. He was overjoyed! It was his at last.

A few years later Hussein came to the United States to study for his Master's degree. While he was studying at Columbia Teachers College in New York City, he met some Christians who invited him to attend church with them. In the summer, they also took him to a children's camp. There he heard an evangelist explain how to receive Christ as Lord and Savior. When the evangelist asked, "If anyone wants to receive Jesus, please stand up," Hussein jumped to his feet.

"You don't have to stand," his Christian friends told him. "The man was speaking to the boys and girls."

"No!" came Hussein's reply, "I want to show that I am receiving Jesus Christ as my Savior." He really knew what the decision meant. He was not just doing it to be polite, as his friends thought.

Shortly after that, we left Afghanistan for a brief home leave, and I was invited to a conference of Afghan believers. It was the first Afghan Christian conference in history, and it was held in New Jersey! Five believers were there from Afghanistan. Each one had thought that he was the only Afghan Christian in the world.

Of these five, Hussein was one.

Each man gave his testimony, and when they had all finished, I saw Afghan culture at work once again.

The man whom they considered their leader, the one they respected the most, began to speak. "I have listened to all your testimonies," he said. "I can see that of the five Afghan Christians here tonight, three have been baptized and two have not. These two should be baptized tonight."

Their leader had spoken. Each Afghan placed his right hand over his heart to indicate, "Yes! We're going to do it with our whole hearts!"

Then one young man spoke up. He had come to Christ while helping my wife and me read the New Testament in Farsi in Kabul.

"I'll be happy to be baptized," he said, "but will someone please tell me what it is?"

So the others explained it to him, and that night Hussein and this new Christian were both baptized by immersion in a family swimming pool in Hawthorne, New Jersey—a pool with underwater lighting set in a beautiful garden.

After Hussein was baptized, he returned to Afghanistan. There he translated a Bible correspondence course into Dari, his own language. He also tape recorded the Gospel, which was then recorded into the two major Afghan tongues. These recordings are being used today among the Afghan refugees.

Hussein died a martyr's death in the prime of life on March 17, 1969. He was poisoned by Muslim zealots because he had become a Christian. I took him from one doctor to another, hoping they could save his life. To no avail. In three days Hussein was dead.

Now that he is in heaven, we don't have to worry that someone will recognize his voice on the recordings. As the Bible says of Abel, "Though he is dead, he is still speaking." Anyone who recognizes his voice cannot hurt him now, because he is in heaven with his Lord.

The Blood of Martyrs

According to Islam's law of apostasy, anyone who leaves the Muslim faith should be killed. In fact, Muslims are taught that if you kill such a person, you yourself are assured of entering paradise—as well as your victim.

Most Afghan Christians have lived under dogged persecution. That's why you find few with a lukewarm faith. It's either all or nothing. Many converts have been beaten, tortured, and martyred.

A Muslim Zealot finds Christ

Yahya Baqui was a zealous Afghan Muslim from Kandahar. In 1855 he made the long pilgrimage to Mecca, but was warned in a dream that he should follow Christ. Not quite knowing what to make of it all, he met Dr. Karl Pfander during a layover in Peshawar on his way home. Dr. Pfander, a missionary, explained to Hajji Yahya Baqui the significance of his dream and baptized him as the first Afghan convert to Christ.

It wasn't long before the new convert's faith was put to the ultimate test. One night Hajji Yahya Baqui was attacked by zealous Muslims who tried to carry out Islamic law, and he was left for dead. Though he bled profusely from seven wounds, he miraculously recovered. But two of his fingers had been cut off. Like the Apostle Paul, he bore scars on his body. He returned to Afghanistan where he witnessed boldly for Christ and was wonderfully protected until he died a natural death.

However, others did not meet with the same fortune as him.

A Notorious Outlaw Turns Preacher

Dilawar Kahn was another Afghan who had been led to Christ through the ministry of Dr. Pfander. He had been a notorious outlaw and border raider with a price on his head. On receiving Christ he gave himself up and claimed his own reward! Then he joined the British Army in India and became a top-ranking officer. His characteristic bravery spilled over into his spiritual life and he did not hesitate to confess Christ publicly.

A military journey brought him to Kabul where he was recognized by an Afghan who had heard him preach in the Peshawar bazaar. Dilawar Khan was arrested and accused before a *qazi* (judge). A copy of a book given to him by Dr. Pfander was used as evidence against him.

The magistrate tore the book in two and condemned Dilawar Khan to be blown to his death from the mouth of a cannon. The King, however, heard of the case and asked to see the book. He inspected it, pronounced it a good book, and set Dilawar Khan free. His freedom didn't last long however. He was sentenced to death and executed by a treacherous ruler in the mountains of Chitral.

An Afghan Becomes A Missionary Doctor

Dr. Theodore Pennell, who started the hospital in Bannu, told the story of another Afghan convert in the early twentieth century. One of the merchants from Laghman in Afghanistan had taken his young son, Jahan Khan with him to India on one of his journeys. The father was stricken with dysentery, and the boy took him to a mission hospital, where for the first time he heard the Gospel story. At first Jahan Khan plugged his ears lest any of the words spoken by the mission doctor defile his faith.

The father, however, did not improve, and was taken to a shrine of a famous saint for healing. Instead he died. His heartbroken son had to bury him near the saint's tomb. Consequently, Jahan Khan found himself an orphan hundreds of miles away from his family.

Dr. Pennell was looking for a helper who knew Pashtu so that he might gain proficiency in that language. Jahan Khan resented the idea of becoming a helper to an infidel, which he thought would jeopardize his Islamic salvation. The young boy only accepted the position after his Muslim patron had laughed at his scruples. "As long as you say your prayers regularly, read the Koran, keep the fast, and do not eat their food lest by any chance there should be swine flesh in it, you have no reason to fear," the Muslim advised Jahan.

After Jahan Kahn had worked at the hospital for a while, an educated Afghan teased him about his inability to read. So the embarrassed boy persuaded the hospital *munshi* (secretary) to give him a lesson every day. Jahan Khan's first readings came from the Pashtu Gospel, which riveted his attention. Instead of the law of "an eye for and eye and a tooth for a tooth," Jahan read about an incredible command that said to forgive your enemies and to love those who persecute you.

Soon, Jahan Khan began to talk constantly about the Gospel message, much to the chagrin of the Muslims. One evening as Dr. Pennell was sitting in his room, he heard shouts from outside, "*O daktar Sahib! O daktar Sahib!*" Two Muslims were beating Jahan, while they tried to stifle his cries by choking him with his turban. But Jahan's close call didn't deter him from reading and talking about Christ's teachings. Shortly after the attempted murder, he publicly confessed he was a Christian.

After his baptism, Jahan had a burning desire to visit his childhood home in Afghanistan and tell his family about his new-found faith. His widowed mother was still living there with his brothers and cousins. Dr. Pennell pointed out the great dangers he faced. At that time it was a capital offense in Afghanistan to convert to Christianity. Jahan Khan, however, would not be dissuaded. Some Gospel copies in Farsi and Pashtu were sewn inside his Afghan garment and off he went.

His mother and brothers received him with delight. But as soon as it was known he was a Christian, the villagers clamored for his life. An uncle, who was himself a *mullah*, managed to appease the angry mob on condition that Jahan leave the country at once. He left his books with some *mullahs* and joined a caravan leaving Afghanistan through the Khyber Pass. But he still wasn't safe. Someone had mixed a poisonous herb in his soup.

Jahan Khan remembered nothing more until the caravan entered Peshawar. It was several days before he was able to make the journey to Bannu, and still longer before he regained his previous health. But his visit had not been without fruit. A brother and two cousins journeyed down from Laghman to Bannu, and while there, one of them requested Christian baptism.

Jahan Khan eventually followed in Dr. Pennell's footsteps and became a doctor. Since there was such a great need for medical work in Karak, he and his devoted wife, who was also a Pathan Christian, started work there. Through their kindness to the sick and the needy they served, the Khans overcame the local anti-Christian prejudice and antagonism.

Dr. Pennell wrote, "I have no greater pleasure than to visit Karak and to see these two faithful workers in their hospital, surrounded by the sick and needy, telling them of the precious sacrifice of Christ."

Faithful Unto Death

Sir Henry Holland, the medical doctor in charge of the Quetta missionary hospital, told of another faithful Afghan convert who had a burning desire to preach the Gospel in Afghanistan. Qazi Abdul Karim, the son of a Muslim judge, worked with the mission hospital in Quetta, and witnessed at every opportunity all along the frontier.

In May of 1906 he traveled to Kandahar where he was arrested and subjected to terrible tortures. Despite this, he would not deny his Christian faith. He refused to repeat the Muslim word of witness, "There is no God but Allah and Mohammed is the apostle of Allah."

Qazi Abdul Karim's nightmare began when a 70-pound chain was placed around his neck and a bridle was put in his mouth. Then he was marched 300 miles from Kandahar to Kabul, where he was abused all along the way. In Kabul, he again was ordered to repeat the Muslim creed. When he refused, his right arm was cut off with a sword.

Again he was ordered to say it.

But once more he refused to betray his Christian faith.

This time he lost his left arm.

He was ordered to repeat the Muslim words of witness a third time.

When he refused, his captors beheaded him.

Twenty-five years later, in 1931, Flora Davidson and Maria Rasmussen were visiting in Mashad, Iran, when an Afghan man came to the home of Dr. and Mrs. William Miller for tea, and told of seeing Qazi Abdul Karim's persecution.

"It was many years ago," he said. "I was a boy of ten or twelve at the time, but I have never been able to forget it. I saw a man tortured and hounded to death for his faith in the streets of Kabul.

"He was a Christian," he continued. "The remembrance of the light of the peace on his face remains with me to this day. I can never forget it. Tell me the secret of it."

The man accepted Christ as his Savior and returned home.

There is a little Christian church in Chaman, on the Baluchistan border of Afghanistan, which today is locked up and unused. Over the fireplace, a framed text honors yet another Afghan martyr, "In memory of Nasrullah Khan who became a Christian on June 11, 1899. He would not deny Christ and was killed by Afghans near Chaman on August 20, 1908. 'He who loses his life for My sake and the Gospel's, the same shall find it.'"

Another young Afghan, Mazzaffar, came to the Lord and was adopted by the Pattersons, a dedicated missionary couple in Pakistan. Mazzaffar traveled to Kabul and witnessed boldly for Christ. When he was caught, a *mullah* forced acid down his throat saying, "You infidel, we will burn the tongue out of your head and you will speak no more about the Son of God in Afghanistan." He died not long afterwards.

And the Blind Shall See

Hafizullah was a blind boy who studied and learned to read Braille in the Institute we had in Herat, Afghanistan. He was one of many who came to Christ and he grew in his faith. One day, he was pushed out of an upstairs window and fell to his death on the stone pavement below. He was killed because he had become a Christian. But we know that although he was blind, he is now with Jesus and sees Him face to face. As the Apostle John wrote, "We know that when He (Jesus Christ) appears, we shall be like Him, for we shall see Him as He is" (I John 3:2b).

They Died On Foreign Soil

Afghan converts have not been the only people to die serving the Lord in Afghanistan. Several Christian foreigners have also met violent deaths and have been buried on Afghan soil. During the mid-1950's, a German athletics instructor was stabbed and killed by a religious fanatic on a Kabul street. He had only been in the country for six weeks.

More recently, on December 30, 1980, the mutilated bodies of Erik and Eeva Barendsen were found on their bedroom floor. Their two children, Asko, age five, and Ulla, age three, were found unhurt. But they had been sitting in the blood of their dead parents for almost a day, and time will tell if they will ever be able to recover from the emotional shock.

Erik Barendsen, a native of Holland, and Eeva, a native of Finland, had met during work at the NOOR Eye Hospital in Kabul. Afghanistan had become home, and when the Russians had allowed a handful of foreigners to stay and work in the country, the Barendsens saw no reason to leave. They continued to stay.

That proved to be fatal. A group of Afghans conducted a rash of murders on December 29 and 30, 1980, to symbolize their disdain for the Russians. It was the one-year anniversary of the invasion. Apparently, the Afghan killers had mistakenly figured that any foreigners left were tied to the Soviet occupation.

These are only some of the Afghan Christian martyrs.

It has been said that the blood of the martyrs is the seed of God's church. If this is true, a glorious church is going to grow one day in Afghanistan.

The Seminary That Goes TO the Students

One of the key people who started Theological Education by Extension (TEE) is Dr. Ralph Winter. He is an amazing person. He established the U.S. Center for World Mission and has been focusing on the unreached peoples of the world. Because of this, he can be called the "Apostle to Unreached Peoples."

I knew Ralph as a student when he attended the first Urbana Student Missionary Convention in Toronto, Ontario in 1946. He planned to go to Afghanistan with us but became so involved with other responsibilities that he couldn't get away. Instead, he went to Guatemala as a missionary.

In Guatemala City he came across a seminary that had been operating for twenty-five years and had graduated more than 200. Yet only ten of their graduates were still in the pastorate. Even worse, the Presbyterian Church in Guatemala had 160 churches with no pastor at all. The seminary was not meeting the needs of the churches.

In studying the problem, Ralph Winter and others discovered that most of the students came to Guatemala City from the rural areas. After they completed seminary, they didn't want to return there but preferred to stay in the city.

"Either we pastor a church in the city or we'll leave the pastorate altogether and take some other job," the graduates said.

So Dr. Winter and two other missionaries, Dr. James Emery and Dr. Ross Kinsler, met together to pray.

"Lord, this is the problem," they prayed. "The seminary is not doing an effective job of training pastors. What can we do?"

Then they had an idea. Instead of having all the students come to the seminary, why not take the seminary out to where the students are! This started Theological Education by Extension (TEE), which has just exploded around the world!

So the seminary took their professors to centers near the 160 churches that had no pastor. The professors began training the lay leaders, teaching them right in their own churches. In time, the seminary trained hundreds of pastors in this way.

Using the seminary campus as a base, the professors traveled from area to area each weekday night. Once a week, these pastors would come to class with their books and completed assignments.

This has now caught on all over the world. In India, for example, more pastors are now being trained by TEE than they are in the seminaries. This holds true in many other countries as well.

God's Blessing on Christianity in Africa

Dr. David Barrett is one the world's leading experts on missions statistics and was formerly a missionary to Kenya from England. He writes:

> *At the beginning of this century, there were only 9.9 million people in the whole continent of Africa who called themselves Christian. But because of God's blessing in missions, by the end of this century, at the present rate, there will be over 393 million people who will call themselves Christians in Africa.*

Dr. Thomas Lambie, whom I knew personally, went as a medical missionary to the Sudan, where he built a hospital. But when Ethiopia began to open up, he transferred there and became one of the pioneers in the Sudan Interior Mission (S.I.M.).

At that time, the law said that only Ethiopian citizens could own land in that nation. This presented a problem for the Mission because they needed land for hospitals, schools and churches. So Dr. Lambie renounced his American citizenship and became an Ethiopian citizen. As a result, all the property was secured in his name, and he became one of the richest men in Ethiopia!

When Italy invaded Ethiopia in the early 1930's, Dr. Lambie and other missionaries were forced to go home, leaving behind only a few Christian nationals. On his return to the States, Dr. Lambie needed an act of Congress to have his citizenship restored.

After Italy was forced to leave Ethiopia, the missionaries returned. To their amazement, they found that those few Christian nationals had multiplied to more than 60,000 believers!

John Eliot: Apostle To Native Americans

Christianity in America owes much to the early missionaries who came to these shores. One of them was John Eliot, who was born in England in 1604. He was a schoolmate and friend of Oliver Cromwell. He studied Greek and Hebrew at Cambridge University and came to New England in 1631, eleven years after the Pilgrims. His goal, like theirs, was to share the Gospel with the native Americans.

The original seal of the Massachusetts Bay Colony had an Indian on it with these words coming out of his mouth, "Come over and help us" from Acts 16:9. Their charter stated that their principal purpose for the plantation was to win the Indian people "to the knowledge and obedience of the only true God and Savior of mankind and the Christian faith." The Massachusetts seal today still has the picture of the same Indian, but because it has become a secular state, the original words from the Scriptures have been blotted out.

John Eliot pastored the church in Roxbury for 58 years, from 1632 to his death in 1690. He and two other pastors translated the Psalms from Hebrew into English poetry for use in their churches and printed *The Bay Psalm Book* in Cambridge, Massachusetts in 1640. This was the first book ever published in North America.

As a pastor, Eliot had a heart of compassion for the poor. Because he was known for giving away much of his salary before he got home to his wife, the church treasurer tied up the coins in a handkerchief, knotting the ends as hard as he could. On the way, Eliot made a pastoral call on a poor widow and her children. He took out the money from his pocket to give her something but could not untie the knots. He therefore gave her the whole handkerchief with all his salary, saying that the Lord must have meant her to have it.

Since his main calling was to reach the native Americans, John Eliot learned the Massachusetts language which belonged to the Algonquin linguistic family. He reduced it to writing, worked out its grammar and then translated the whole Bible into it. This was published in 1663 as the first Bible printed in the New World.

In 1645 he started the Roxbury Latin School, which is still operating today. In 1989 the alumni purchased a copy of Eliot's Massachusetts Indian Bible for $300,000 and presented it to the school in honor of their founder.

Cotton Mather, another famous New England pastor, wrote Eliot's biography called, *The Life of the Renowned John Eliot*. This was published in Boston in 1691, the year after his death. In this, he wrote that Eliot firmly believed that the Indians would be eternally lost if the Gospel were hidden from them. That is what drove him to finish translating the Scriptures into their language. "The Bible is the Word of life. They must have it," he would say.

Eliot led thousands of native Americans to Christ, and trained some of them as pastors and teachers. After he preached to them in their own language, he would give them an opportunity to ask questions. One of them inquired, "Does God understand the Indians' prayers?" He answered, "God made Indians. He knows all about you. Of course He knows your language and understands every word. He definitely hears your prayers."

Another asked him about faith in God. "How do we believe what eyes cannot see?"

He replied, "When you see a big wigwam, do you think the raccoons built it? Or the foxes? Or that it built itself? Certainly not. Look at the house of this great world. Look at the sun, the moon, the stars. Doesn't it look as though a very powerful wise Being built it? We cannot see Him with our eyes, but we look at His work."

John Eliot gathered the converted Indians into fourteen Praying Towns in Massachusetts and Connecticut. He organized these towns on the Biblical model of the children of Israel in the wilderness, where Moses appointed leaders of tens, fifties and of hundreds. He had the Indians elect their own leaders. They also had their own schools and churches. Instead of church bells, they called them to their services with Indian drums. No wonder Nathaniel Hawthorne wrote in his book, *Grandfather's Chair*, "Since the first days of Christianity, there has been no man more worthy to be numbered in the brotherhood of the Apostles than Eliot."

Through John Eliot's friendship with Oliver Cromwell and others, the English Parliament passed an act establishing the first Protestant Missionary Society in 1649. This helped support Eliot's work among the Indians as well as publishing the books he wrote for them. In 1650 he wrote *The Christian Commonwealth*, on which the United States Constitution is based.

In 1990, for the tricentennial anniversary of his death, we had a Vision Conference in Roxbury, where he is buried. Hundreds attended it in the Twelfth Baptist Church there. Then we had a prayer march through Roxbury to one of three churches that are named in memory of John Eliot. The City of Boston gave us a police escort. The prayer march then continued to the old cemetery, where we found his tomb. At the celebration we had an evangelical Christian Indian Chief, John Maracle, from the Mohawk Tribe who marched in his native American Indian outfit. He led in prayer beside the grave asking the Lord to raise many more like John Eliot to take the Gospel to the unreached native Americans as well as others.

Following his prayer, a black lady from Roxbury came up and talked personally to Chief Maracle. She had followed the crowd into the cemetery. Chief Maracle then put his arm around her and led her in private prayer. Afterwards I asked him if he wouldn't mind sharing what this was about. He said that her son had just been shot and killed in Roxbury three days before. And he had prayed for her, asking God's comfort on her. What a sight this was to see a Christian Indian Chief with his arm around a grief-stricken black mother, comforting her!

I wonder whether John Eliot saw this from heaven and rejoiced.

Samuel Zwemer: Apostle to Islam

Dr. Samuel Zwemer is often called the "Apostle to Islam." Without doubt, I believe he was the greatest missionary to Muslims in history.

He traveled all over the Muslim world in his missionary zeal to bring them to Christ, studying Islam as it was practiced from Arabia and Iran to the ends of China. His wife was a wonderful woman of God from Australia. Amy Wilkes was her maiden name.

Amy had a wonderful mastery of the English language, as did Dr. Zwemer. There is an amusing story about her when she was in Iran. While enjoying coffee with some of the missionary ladies, she asked one of them whether she drank "coffee at night with impunity," and the lady replied, "No, I take cream and sugar."

Dr. Zwemer had been a professor of missions at Princeton Theological Seminary for four years when my parents returned from Iran on furlough in 1933. I came back to the States with them. We lived on the edge of the campus. So I had the opportunity to know Dr. Zwemer personally.

In 1939, my father returned to the States from Iran. The Second World War had started, and Russia was occupying northern Iran. It was impossible for him to go back again. Therefore, when Dr. Zwemer retired as Professor of Missions at Princeton Seminary, my father was appointed to succeed him.

After his retirement, Dr. Zwemer lived on the thirteenth floor of an apartment building on Fifth Avenue. My father made many trips back and forth to New York to see him while writing Dr. Zwemer's biography entitled, *Apostle to Islam*. Although retired, Dr. Zwemer would return to give guest lectures at Princeton while I was in seminary. It was very exciting to hear him speak.

Dr. Zwemer had such a sense of humor. If you read about what he did in Arabia it was no wonder the people loved him.

One time he went to Jeddah, which is the port thirty-five miles from Mecca. He and his partner James Cantine were planning to launch the Arabian Mission.

When Dr. Zwemer reached Jeddah, he rented a room and started selling Bibles. Before long he was arrested and put in prison.

Now I had heard him say before that he used to envy the Apostle Paul for having so much time in prison to write the New Testament.

"I seem to have so much to do," said Dr. Zwemer, "that I am not able to spend the time on writing and praying that Paul did." So when he was sent to prison, he was glad for all the free time he would have for prayer.

Sharing his prison cell was a Christian from Egypt. On the wall of the cell was a huge picture of an Arab. The two Christians prayed for this man for a period of time. Then they tired of praying for him and used his picture as a target for throwing spitballs. It was a game to see who could hit the man's nose.

Finally, after three days in prison, Dr. Zwemer was released. No more would he envy the Apostle Paul for all that free time in prison, he said, because he now saw how boring it could really be.

Before leaving Jeddah, he rented space for a Bible bookstore, later inviting Jenny de Mayer, a Christian nurse from Russia, to set up her medical dispensary there. She posted Bible verses all over the walls as a witness to her patients.

Dr. Zwemer was always interested in learning more about Islam. Once he saw a man selling Zam-Zam water. Zam-Zam was the name of the well in Mecca from which pilgrims drink water. So Dr. Zwemer bought this "holy" water.

On the ship home, someone found out that he had bought it and the Muslims on board became excited when they heard that this non-Muslim had water from the sacred well, Zam-Zam. The captain heard about it and when Dr. Zwemer realized that they were going to take the water away from him, he went to his cabin, poured the Zam-Zam water into another container and then filled the bottle with water right from the tap.

The captain demanded that he turn the bottle of "holy water" over to him. Dr. Zwemer handed him the substitute and the captain quaffed it down, saying that Zam-Zam water was good for curing anything. Dr. Zwemer held on to the real Zam-Zam water and had it tested when he got back. He found that it was just filled with all kinds of pollutants.

Peter Zwemer: Mistaken for Jesus

Dr. Samuel Zwemer's brother Peter also served as missionary to the Muslims, but died while still a young man. The two brothers, together with James Cantine, were pioneers in reaching the Muslims and were greatly loved by the people.

When Samuel Zwemer was a senior at Hope College in Holland, Michigan, he went to hear a talk by Robert Wilder, the man used by God to start the Student Volunteer Movement. Robert Wilder was visiting college campuses to recruit students for missions. He had them sign the statement, "God helping me, I purpose to be a foreign missionary."

At this meeting, Robert Wilder displayed a large map of India. Standing prominently in front was a metronome, used to keep time in music. Wilder said that every time it ticked, someone in India died without having heard the Gospel.

As soon as Samuel Zwemer heard that, he knew he had to go and tell people about Christ! No sooner had Dr. Wilder finished speaking—while the metronome was still ticking—than he rushed to the front and signed the pledge.

Dr. Zwemer wanted to go to the most difficult mission field in the world. After some research, he decided that the Muslims in Saudi Arabia were the most resistant to the Gospel. So of course that's where he was determined to go. But no mission board would send him.

"You'll be killed!" they told him. "We'll be sending you to die."

Because of this response, Samuel Zwemer and James Cantine set up their own organization, calling it the "Arabian Mission." Each one went to churches and raised support for the other.

"If God calls you to go to a place like Arabia and no mission board will send you," Samuel said, "why, bore a hole through the board and go anyway!"

The two men first went to Beirut and then Cairo, where they learned Arabic. Then they traveled all around the Arabian peninsula, looking for a place to start their mission.

After scouting the area thoroughly, even in the inland regions of Arabia, they set up their mission in Busra. They also established stations in Kuwait, the island of Bahrain, and in Muscat, Oman.

Peter Zwemer, Samuel's brother and a wonderful young man of God, came to Muscat as a missionary and established an orphanage for African boys.

While Peter was in Muscat, the British Navy captured and held a slave ship in that port, since the British had outlawed slavery. The ship had left Africa and was on its way to Saudi Arabia to sell the slaves—thirty-five little black boys—who had already been branded. After capturing the ship, the British didn't know what to do with these thirty-five boys.

So Peter Zwemer made the British an offer.

"I'll take care of them," he said.

He took the thirty-five little black boys, housed them, provided them with beds, food, and clothing. He even started a school for them. He taught them the Bible in addition to English and other subjects.

While still a young man, Peter Zwemer took sick and died and was buried in Muscat.

Years later Samuel Zwemer returned to Muscat. Preaching in Arabic, he told the people about Jesus Christ.

"Oh, but we know him," someone interrupted.

"Oh no, you've got me wrong," Dr. Zwemer said. "This is someone who lived many, many years ago."

He went on to tell them how Jesus Christ loved little children, how he had done many good things for people and had even given His life for them.

"We know him!" another one shouted.

"No, you don't," Dr. Zwemer insisted. "He lived a long time ago, before you were born." And he continued talking about Jesus.

The people raised their hands once again.

"But we do know him!"

And they proceeded to describe Peter Zwemer!

Like Jesus, Peter had loved children. Like Jesus, he had had compassion for people and had done so many good things for them. And like Jesus, he had given his life for them.

What a wonderful thing. To be mistaken for Jesus!

Chapter 6
Personal Reminiscences

Lost In An Airplane Over Afghanistan

"If you don't know God, come to know him by his power."
(Afghan Proverb)

Glancing at my watch, 6:05 p.m., August 31, 1955, I knew something was wrong. We should have been preparing to land by now. I peered out of the Iran Air DC 3 window, expecting to see the familiar barren mountains surrounding Afghanistan's capital and largest city—Kabul. But below stretched pine forests, valleys and rugged mountains as far as the eye could see.

Suddenly I realized we were lost! Kabul was at least one hundred miles from the nearest forest.

Sitting at the controls of the plane were two Americans. The pilot had never been in Afghanistan, and the co-pilot was serving as guide without the aid of today's sophisticated navigational equipment. This was only his second flight through the Afghan skies.

Somewhere during the course of the scheduled one-hour and forty-five minute flight, our pilot had made a wrong turn. I guessed from the topography of the terrain below that we were probably over the Afghan province of Khost, headed toward Nuristan and the Russian-Chinese border.

I swallowed hard. We were flying without any place to land over the jagged Central Asian wilderness.

Towering mountains soon dwarfed our small prop plane, with its unpressurized cabin. Banks of pink, billowy clouds loomed thousands of feet above us on the distant horizon. Then the twilight completely disappeared over the edge of the earth behind us. We seemed to be flying into an endless sea of blackness.

I was on this flight because I had accompanied a group of Afghan students to Tehran, Iran. They had boarded a westbound plane to continue their long journey to universities in the United States. Now, I was returning to Kabul to continue my teaching and administrative duties at Habibia College, one of Afghanistan's oldest and most respected schools for high school age boys.

Lost in my own thoughts, I wondered what else could go wrong. Mechanical difficulties had caused a two-hour delay in our departure that morning from Tehran's Mehrabad Airport. Then Iranian customs officials at Zahidan, near the southwestern tip of Afghanistan, had delayed us even further when they insisted that all baggage be taken off the plane and inspected.

The sun was already hanging low in the sky when we had reached our next stop—Kandahar, Afghanistan's largest southern city. We had dropped off about a half-dozen passengers, and before long we were speeding down the Kandahar runway for the final 300-mile leg of our flight.

At 4:20 p.m., our pilot had been confident that by dusk we would be taxiing toward the small Kabul terminal. But somewhere over Ghanzi, he had followed a road heading northeast, paralleling the Pakistan border, instead of taking the northerly route to Kabul.

The more I thought about it, the more I realized the next few hours could very well be my last on earth.

I knew there were no night landing facilities in Afghanistan, or anywhere else within range. I also knew that the front baggage compartments were stashed with four-gallon cans filled with aviation fuel for the return trip—a necessity since fuel was not always available. A crash meant certain death in a blazing inferno.

I sensed a deep spiritual responsibility to speak with people on the plane about their relationship with God. Most passengers I talked to were very receptive. One American, however, cut me short saying, "Don't talk to me about that. When my time comes, it comes. And that's all there is to it!" He then turned away and continued to stare out the window into the night.

I then started a conversation with the Iranian steward. He responded: "I've been to Mecca. Doesn't that make me all right?"

I told him that the important issue now was not where he had been, but where he stood now in his relationship with God. If he repented of his sins and believed that Jesus had died on the cross in his place, then he would receive God's forgiveness. The steward seemed very receptive to what I was saying because he, like the others on the plane, was very frightened. He knew that the odds of coming out alive were against us.

A little later the steward gave me permission to enter the cockpit. I learned that the only radio contact the pilot and co-pilot had had was with Tehran, about 1300 miles to the west, and Karachi, Pakistan, an equal distance to the south. (Afghanistan airports were not yet radio-equipped.) The pilot banked the plane sharply to the left, completed a 180-degree turn, and started to follow the flight log in reverse.

It was the only solution he could think of.

When I mentioned I was a Christian minister, the co-pilot glanced over his shoulder and said, "Use all the influence you've got!"

"I'm praying," I answered. "And I know that God is in charge."

I returned to my seat and began to pray. I placed the fifteen people on the plane in God's hands. Then I pulled my Bible from my briefcase and wrote this note on the inside front cover:

Dearest Betty, Nancy, Christy, and Martin,
  Our pilots have lost their way, and it appears that we will crash. I am writing this farewell message in case my Bible is found in the wreckage. I love you more than words can tell.
  Put Jesus first throughout your life and serve Him faithfully in every way you can. I look forward to seeing you again soon in Heaven.
    Your loving husband and dad,
    Christy

I had just finished signing the note when from the corner of my eye I caught a glimpse of something coming up over the left wing. A beautiful full moon was rising over the eastern horizon, illuminating the mountains and valleys. God brought this miracle of timing just when we needed it. We had finally come out of the ominous clouds into clearer night air. The pilot then kept flying by moonlight.

I went back to the cockpit and scouted the silver landscape below. The terrain looked vaguely familiar. I soon recognized a village I had driven through only ten days earlier when I had traveled the bumpy road from Kabul to Kandahar for the funeral of an American engineer. He had drowned in the Helmand River while helping to build a dam.

"That town down there is Qalat!" I said to the pilot over the engine's roar. I remembered that Qalat had a spring of water which stands within an adobe fort on a hill like an acropolis. The co-pilot checked the map and found our location. From there we headed for Kandahar.

My prayers had been answered.

8:30 p.m. We could see the glow of Kandahar's lights in the distance. But the joy I felt was short-lived. Some quick arithmetic told me we had been airborne for more than four hours. We would soon run out of fuel.

No sooner had this thought crossed my mind than the co-pilot spoke up: "We've got to get the airport lit up before we can land!"

"I don't think there is so much as one light bulb at the airfield," I replied softly, hating to reveal the gravity of the situation.

The pilot turned to look at me. "If we can't get it lit up, we'll have to continue flying until we reach Iran!" Then he added solemnly, "But we don't have enough fuel to make it."

How ironic! Even though we had jerry tins of extra gasoline on board, there was no way to fuel the plane while in flight.

Soon we reached the outskirts of Kandahar, and I sighted the Morrison-Knutsen Construction camp. This company had been contracted by the Afghanistan and United States governments to build an irrigation system in Afghanistan's Helmand Valley. During the 1950's, two dams were erected and hundreds of miles of irrigation ditches were dredged in an effort to help the Afghans produce more food in their arid climate. Patterned after the Tennessee Valley Authority, this project had involved hundreds of Americans at one time or another.

I pointed out the location of the camp to the pilots.

"Why don't we fly low over the camp?" I suggested. "Planes don't fly into Kandahar at night so the noise of the engines will attract attention. The construction workers may realize we're in trouble and figure out a way to help."

The pilot made three passes as low as he dared.

Within minutes, many jeeps, cars, and trucks at the site were racing to the airfield. Light from their headlights flooded the runway as the vehicles lined up on each side of the gravel strip!

The landing was perfect!

By the time the flight attendant could lift the latch and open the cabin door, our "welcoming committee" had gathered to greet us. Several of us couldn't wait for the steward to roll down the portable stairs. We leaped out the open door to the ground below, into the midst of the jubilant American workers. No one had ever looked so welcome as these men who had saved our lives!

One husky American engineer recognized me.

"Christy, you mean to say you were on that plane!" he said incredulously. Then he engulfed me in a bear hug I shall never forget. We had become acquainted on my recent visit to Kandahar. Not only had I conducted funeral services for his friend, but I had baptized his daughter as well.

Morrison-Knutsen's director, T.Y. Johnson, invited all the passengers and crew to a steak dinner at the construction camp. To top it off, they served strawberry shortcake for dessert. Our unexpected hosts also rolled out every spare cot and bed on the grounds, doing their best to convert their simple accommodations into a first-class hotel. The Waldorf-Astoria it was not. But we did not care. We were all happy just to be alive.

The next day, September 1, 1955, dawned bright and clear. After a hearty breakfast, the construction crew chauffeured us all back to the airport. They refused to take a penny for their hospitality.

My mind again began to wander as we gained altitude and the DC 3 propellers spun us toward Kabul for the second time.

Never had I been more grateful for answered prayer. God's words in Psalm 50:16 were even more meaningful now:

I want you to trust Me in your times of trouble,
so I can rescue you and you can give Me glory.

Time and time again, God had reaffirmed my decision to bring my wife Betty to this mountainous, out-of-the-way country in the heart of Central Asia where our three children had been born and raised. I had been ready to die to go to be with Jesus. But the miracle of the previous evening had confirmed that God indeed wanted me working and living among these freedom-loving people in Afghanistan, where later we saw the Lord give spiritual fruit and had many other experiences of God's gracious providence.

The "Hidden Highway" Into Afghanistan

I had never thought of myself as a tentmaker until after we were already in Afghanistan. I didn't understand the concept of self-supporting witness then. However, since missionaries were not allowed at that time, the only way to get there was to take a job.

Then one day, I happened to be reading in my Bible in Acts 18:3, about the Apostle Paul and I saw that this was what he had done.

Then the idea began to take shape in my mind. This was the "hidden highway" into Afghanistan. I suddenly realized that I too was a tentmaker!

Because of this, I wrote the book *Today's Tentmakers*, published by Tyndale Press in 1979. One of the men there told me, "Don't be disappointed but missionary books don't sell." I almost asked if the Bible were not a missionary book. But I kept quiet and prayed that the Lord would confound his counsel. They have had to reprint this more than eight times with a total of over 50,000 copies.

In her book *The Hidden Highway*, Flora Davidson writes that even though we don't know how God is going to open the way into Afghanistan and into the hearts of the people, we know that there is a way. But so far it had been hidden. It turned out that this hidden highway was tentmaking, because that's the way the Christians got in, as teachers, engineers, diplomats, peace corps workers, doctors and nurses.

It all came about this way.

In 1947 Pakistan separated from India after the British pulled out of the Indian subcontinent. Now Afghanistan, which had been British-controlled, was free to develop its own foreign policy.

At that time, 97 percent of the Afghan people couldn't read or write. To get ahead, they needed an education. But the country did not have enough teachers. So Afghanistan advertised in other countries, seeking teachers.

Friends of mine found a notice on a bulletin board at Columbia Teachers College in New York City. We duplicated it and sent it to InterVarsity chapters and staff in the U.S. and Canada, saying, "Here's an opportunity to get into Afghanistan as a teacher."

"Here lies the man who tried to rush the East"

I too applied to the Afghan Embassy in Washington, D.C. early in 1947 to go as a teacher.

Before applying for a teaching position in Afghanistan, I had been Missionary Secretary for InterVarsity in the United States and Canada. I resigned from this position when I applied to go to Afghanistan as a teacher.

Not having heard anything from the Afghan Embassy, I thought I should make plans just in case this didn't work out. So I applied to the University of Edinburgh in Scotland to pursue my Ph.D. in Islamic studies, and I was accepted.

A Time of Preparation

Two years after completing my degree, in 1949, I returned to the United States. It would be another two years before I finally received permission to go to Afghanistan.

During this waiting period, I took post-doctoral courses at Columbia Teachers College in both linguistics and teaching English as a second language. This training helped me tremendously. I was also able to pastor a few churches here in the States, which was good experience. Later, when we started the house church in Afghanistan, I knew how to organize it.

On my return to the States from Scotland, Betty and I became engaged. She studied at a Biblical Seminary in New York City. We were married in 1950.

After our marriage, my mother gave me some advice.

"Christy," she said, "when Betty says, 'I'm hungry,' what are you going to do? It's great to plan on going to Afghanistan, but now you have a wife! You have to feed her, so you need to get a job."

So while I was waiting, I applied for a position as a youth pastor at a church in Pennsylvania. But they wanted me to sign a contract for two years.

"I'm sorry," I said. "I've applied to go to Afghanistan. I want to be free to go whenever the door opens."

"If that's the case," they said, "we can't accept you."

When Dr. Herbert Mekeel, of the first Presbyterian Church in Schenectady, New York, heard that I was unemployed, he asked me to come and help him out with one of the daughter churches he had started. I said the same thing to him, that I believed God wanted me to go whenever the door opened.

"Wonderful!" said Dr. Mekeel. "Whenever God opens the door for you to go to Afghanistan, that's when we want you to go!" He had a great heart for missions. "Come for a few weeks, a few months, a few years, or whatever it is. Then when the door to Afghanistan opens for you, you'll have praying people behind you." And that's exactly what happened.

Dr. Mekeel was a marvelous man of God.

"Look, you need to start a church in your area," he would say to the people in his congregation. "I want you to leave this church and go out and start another one. You can come to the evening service here, but not the morning one!"

Dr. Mekeel planted about twelve churches as well as founded a Christian conference grounds and a camp for boys and girls. He had more than 350 young people from that church go into full-time Christian service!

My wife and I were there for only eight months, but that church has kept me as *minister extra-muros*, or minister outside-the-walls, for over forty years. I'm a regular minister of that church even now! Whenever we came back to the United States on a furlough, that church would welcome us with open arms.

On one of our home leaves the pastor, Dr. Mekeel, who had never been to the Holy Land, entrusted the church to me for three months while he traveled in the footsteps of the Apostle Paul. On another furlough we had, he asked me take over the church while he went to

Scotland to study for three months. Even now, several times a year the church invites me to come back to preach.

From that one church, also, about a dozen people came to work with us in Afghanistan.

The present senior pastor, Rev. Michael Alford, who is a graduate of Gordon-Conwell, continues to carry on the good work.

Signing the contract to serve in Afghanistan

Finally, after more than four years of waiting, the door to Afghanistan opened!

I went to Washington along with my father, who had just returned from there with Dr. Laubach. I told the Afghan Ambassador that I was a pastor. He didn't clearly understand that term because at that time there were no Christians in Afghanistan. But he got the idea that I was some sort of religious person.

"Will it be all right for me to go as a teacher even though I am a Christian pastor?" I asked.

His answer was very interesting.

"Most of our teachers are Muslim priests," he answered. "So it will be good to have a Christian priest teaching our young people." So he accepted me.

However, something else in the contract puzzled me. There was a statement saying I agreed not to interfere with business and/or politics and/or religion. I asked the Ambassador what that meant.

"If I go to Afghanistan as a teacher and a student asks me a religious question, does this mean I'm not allowed to answer?"

"Absolutely not!" he said. "A teacher is supposed to answer! That's what a teacher is for—to answer questions. We put that in because we had fanatical Muslim groups going in and starting riots. That's what we don't want. But as for answering a student's question, why, a teacher must answer a student's question."

So I signed the contract.

Although the Afghan government paid my way to Afghanistan, there was no money for Betty's air fare. They didn't give anything for a dependent! So Betty and I prayed to the Lord, "What shall we do? We only have enough money for one ticket."

I went to New York City to see a Christian travel agent and I explained the problem to him. I said, "I have $880 for one ticket and to ship my things, but how can my wife go?"

"I think I have the answer," he replied. "In Brazil, the exchange rate is such that I can get two tickets there for the price of one. I will cable some missionaries who are down in Brazil and ask them to buy two Pan American tickets. There's nothing wrong with doing this. They're coming to the States and they can bring the tickets with them." So for the price of one ticket, we got two!

This was Thursday and we were leaving on Monday. That evening I received a telephone call from Washington, D.C. It was the Secretary at the Afghan Embassy.

"The Ambassador wants to see you again. Something has come up," he said.

"I'm sorry," I said, "but I had planned to go to New York on Friday to ship my books by surface freight."

"It looks as if you're not going to Afghanistan after all!"

"Why not?"

"I can't tell you over the telephone. You'll have to come and see the Ambassador personally."

So that night I telephoned all my Christian friends.

"I don't know what has happened, but please pray. Something has come up."

The Church in Schenectady had held a farewell service for us and had commissioned us to go to Afghanistan. They had said their goodbyes and had presented us with gifts. Now to hear that we were not going would be a terrible anti-climax.

Despite the uncertainty, my father went to New York on Friday and shipped my books by freight. My wife's parents had come from Canada to see us off, and they drove Betty and me to Washington. At the Afghan Embassy, they sat in the car outside praying while I went in because we didn't know what the problem was.

When I saw the Ambassador, he said, "I'm concerned about the religious situation in Afghanistan."

"Well, Your Excellency," I said. "I was born and raised in Iran and I understand the religious situation in that part of the world. I don't want to cause any trouble. I want to help the people."

"Oh, if that's the case, we'll be happy to have you go. I'll be right back!" He hurried off and came back with twelve brand-new Arrow shirts. "Will you please take these to the Prime Minister for me?"

Although our luggage already weighed more than the allowable limit, I said we'd be happy to take them. Then he served me tea and everything seemed fine.

My trial at the State Department

Now, I was also waiting for the State Department to renew my passport. Although I had applied for this about a month earlier, I still had not heard from them. So I said to Betty and her parents, "Now that we're here in Washington and I've seen the Afghan Ambassador and everything seems all right, let's go to the State Department to see if they've sent my passport to the wrong address."

Upon arriving there, I found I faced a very serious problem. When they found out who I was, they took me to see the head of the whole Passport Division, a lady by the name of Mrs. Shipley. She sat behind an imposing desk in a huge office.

"Sit down, please," she said. So I did. "Are you going to Afghanistan to preach the Gospel?"

"Well, Mrs. Shipley," I answered, "I know they don't have freedom of religion there now, but sometime if they do, I would count it a privilege to tell the people about my Lord."

She hit the desk with her fist.

"This is what we've been afraid of!" she said.

Then she refused to give me my passport and sent me off to see a number of different people in the Department.

"It is very foolish for a Christian pastor to go to this Muslim country right on the border of Communist China and Russia," they said. "This is very unwise. It will be very dangerous for you. You must not go!" Well, I knew the Lord had called me there.

One American official asked me whether I had seen the Afghan Ambassador or not. I told him that I had.

"What did he say?" he queried.

I replied that he had told me it would be all right to go.

He then phoned to check this out.

By this time it was getting late and they were about to close the office. Now, if you're an American citizen, the State Department cannot refuse to give you a passport unless you have advocated the overthrow of the U.S. Government by force. Well, I had never done that. So after trying to talk me out of this, they finally relented and gave me my passport.

As a result, we were able to leave on Monday.

When I arrived in Afghanistan, one of the things they had me do was teach English to the diplomats. So besides teaching in the regular school, I also taught a course in the Ministry of Foreign Affairs for those who were going to English-speaking countries. I made friends with the Afghan diplomats, and they told me what had happened behind the scenes.

"You know," one of them said, "the State Department told us not to accept you. But we didn't listen. We accepted you anyway."

I thanked God for their spirit of independence.

"After you, Marco Polo"

We flew from New York to Peshawar, Pakistan. From there, it was only another 180 miles to Kabul, but the road was terrible, covered with large river bed stones. The only transportation was a truck that had been converted into a bus, with hard wooden seats. At that time, we were also expecting our first child in four months. I knew that it would be foolish for Betty to ride in that truck. It would have taken two days to make the bumpy trip.

We were in the Deans hotel in Peshawar, praying, when a man came up to me during dinner and called me by name.

"Has the CIA traced me here?" I wondered.

But the man said, "I just want you to know there's a brand-new Chevrolet station wagon with a chauffeur ready to drive you and your wife to Kabul tomorrow morning." I couldn't believe my ears. I had no idea who he was!

After we finished our dinner, I went to the hotel manager.

"Excuse me, sir, who was that man who came and spoke to me?"

"Oh, he's from the United Nations," the manager replied. "He just arrived from Afghanistan with a chauffeur-driven station wagon and asked me if any UN specialists had come in. I pointed you out."

"But I'm not with the United Nations," I said. Then I located the room where this UN representative was staying.

"Sir," I told him when I found him, "I appreciate so much your coming to our table and offering us the use of a car because my wife and I are looking for transportation to Kabul. But I must tell you that I'm not with the United Nations."

"Oh, you aren't?" he said.

"No," I replied.

"I tell you what," he said. "The car has to go back anyway. You and your wife go and take anyone you want along with you." So we went and found the UN specialist they had mistaken me for and invited him and his wife to go with us!

This is how the Lord enabled us to travel to Kabul in one day.

At that time, Afghanistan was very suspicious of foreigners. They thought that all outsiders had a hidden motive. Therefore, they assigned two secret police to every foreigner who came in—one to watch him during the day and one to watch him at night. So I had two secret policemen assigned to me.

Praying for my Afghan students

I taught in the government schools, and in each of my classes, the police had paid one of the students to tell them if I said anything that was out of line. Some students would put up their hand to ask a question.

"Sir, what do you think of Mohammed?"

"Excuse me, this is an English class," I would answer. "You can ask that of your theology professor who is a Muslim priest."

The students also loved to cheat. They saw nothing wrong in that. The sin was to get caught. So I would have to place their chairs as far apart as possible and walk around during the whole examination. The exams were three hours long, but I would turn it into a prayer meeting. I would pray for each student by name.

"Lord, help this student to hear the Gospel." And I would go through the whole class that way. The next time round, I would pray: "Lord, when this student hears the Gospel, open his heart to believe." I would have a wonderful prayer meeting.

We had other Christian teachers there as well, and we would meet together early in the morning to pray for our students and the country. So even though there was terrible religious oppression, still we had the freedom to pray!

We also had the freedom to show the fruit of the Holy Spirit: love, joy, peace, and so on. The Scriptures say: "Against these there is no law." No country can say you can't love, or you can't be joyful, or you can't have peace! And people saw the difference in the lives of Christians in Afghanistan.

Jesus Said, "I Will Build My Church"

"When Satan fell to earth, he fell in Kabul." So goes an oft-quoted Afghan saying.

When we arrived in Kabul, we felt the power of evil very strongly. We sensed oppressive forces surrounding us on all sides.

We started a house church in our home and, since I had been ordained during World War II to become a chaplain in the U.S. Navy and had worked in churches, I was asked to serve as the pastor. We would draw the curtains so no one would know that we were worshiping the Lord, the situation was so oppressive.

At first, our church was made up of the Christian teachers who had come to Afghanistan as tentmakers. There were also Christians from the various embassies and from the United Nations. finally, so many came that we didn't have enough room to pack everyone in our home, which was small. I would stand in the doorway and preach to people in four rooms!

Then in 1959 I heard that President Dwight D. Eisenhower was coming to Afghanistan on his Asian tour.

Many don't realize that former General Eisenhower was baptized after he became President.

His godly mother had named him Dwight after Dwight L. Moody, the great evangelist whom she highly respected. But he had never been baptized nor joined a church. When he got to the White House, he requested baptism and joined the National Presbyterian Church in Washington, D.C. on confession of faith. This was pastored by Dr. Edward Elson, whom the President knew while the former was a chaplain in the U.S. Army.

A mosque had been built in Washington for Muslim diplomats, and President Eisenhower had been invited to the opening. So I wrote to Dr. Elson, whom I knew, and asked him to forward this message to the President.

"Since a mosque has been built for the Muslim diplomats in Washington," I said, "on a reciprocal basis, we should have a church built here in Kabul for the Christian diplomats. We have no place large enough where we can gather. Would you please ask the President to request permission for this from the King when he visits Afghanistan?"

President Eisenhower agreed and when he was in Kabul, he asked the King's permission to build a church. Finally, the Afghan Government gave us the authorization.

We did not have an architect, but God worked in a wonderful way. The president of the Architects Association of New Zealand, Mr. Thomas Haughey, was a Christian who came to visit Afghanistan because he was interested in the Lord's work there. We asked him if he would be willing to draw up the architectural plans, and he readily agreed. The plans were beautiful.

Then we set out to raise money for the construction. People from all over the world sent money for this church.

A Christian lady from a Communist country, whose husband was a diplomat in Kabul, slipped into our home one day.

"I'm so glad that the Afghan Government has given you permission to build a church," she said. "I'm a Christian but I can't come to worship there because the secret police from my country watch me all the time. However, I want to make a contribution."

Students in Korea heard about the plans for the church and they sent money. A little church in Japan, with only seventeen members, sent money. Then some of the blind in Afghanistan, who had come to Christ, gave some of the few coins they had.

Nevertheless, we still were about $20,000 short.

Finally, after prayer, we received a phone call from an American lady from Vermont, who had arrived unexpectedly in Afghanistan. She called me from the Kabul airport.

"I would like to meet with you." So I drove out to meet her.

"I understand that you have permission to build a church."

"Yes, we do," I replied.

"Please let me see the plans," she said. I showed them to her. "How much money do you still need to complete the building?"

I told her we needed $20,000.

"My husband has gone to be with the Lord, and my relatives are taken care of, so I have been traveling around the world giving away my money before I go to heaven. I want to lay up treasures there. I don't want the government to get my money after I die nor do I want my relatives to fight over it. I want to invest it for eternity. I'll provide that $20,000." And she did!

And so in 1970 Afghanistan got its first evangelical Christian church building on its own soil. At its dedication, the cornerstone carved in beautiful Afghan alabaster read: "To the glory of God, 'Who loves us and has freed us from our sins by His blood,' this building is dedicated as 'a house of prayer for all nations' in the reign of His Majesty Zahir Shah, May 17, 1970 AD, 'Jesus Christ Himself being the Chief Cornerstone.'"

Three years later the building was demolished *(see Chapter 8)*.

Swimming To Afghanistan

Dr. William Miller is a marvelous prayer warrior. He is ninety-nine years old now (1992) and lives in Philadelphia, Pennsylvania. When Dr. Miller was in seminary with my father, he hung a map of the world over his bed and would kneel and pray:

"Lord, I'll serve you anywhere in the world that you want me to. Show me where you want me to go."

God called Dr. Miller to Iran, at the border of Afghanistan, to the city of Mashad, that had just opened up to Christian work. There he spent forty-three years and led hundreds of Muslims to Christ.

After Dr. Miller had received the answer to his prayer and knew exactly where God wanted him to serve, he began praying for others. As Jesus said, "Pray to the Lord of the harvest that He will thrust forth laborers into His harvest."

Even before he went to Iran, Dr. Miller encouraged more than a hundred young people to go out as missionaries to other parts of the world. My father and mother went to Iran because of Dr. Miller. Another he encouraged to go was Dr. Philip Howard, the father of missionaries Dr. David Howard and Elisabeth Elliot. Dr. David Howard went to Columbia with the Latin America Mission, then headed up two Urbana Student Missionary Conventions. He also led the Lausanne Pattaya Conference in Thailand in 1980 and has directed the World Evangelical Fellowship headquarters in Singapore. Elisabeth Elliot served among the Auca Indians in Ecuador, where her husband Jim was martyred.

When Dr. Miller was in Iran in 1921, the year that I was born there in Tabriz, he went to the large stream that divides Afghanistan and Iran called the Helmand River. It was out in the middle of the wilderness with no guards or anyone around. He swam across the river to the Afghan side, where he picked some grass and swam back. He then enclosed the grass in letters and sent them to Christian friends.

"Here are some of the firstfruits of Afghanistan!" he wrote.

That turned out to be a prophetic word since many of the stories in this book tell about Afghans who have come to Christ and through Him have obtained eternal life.

"Sight" for the Blind

God used Betty to help start a work with the blind. It all began in 1959 when our American visitor, Johnny Morris, found a little blind boy sitting aimlessly outside his uncle's vegetable shop in Kabul and brought him to our home.

"We must do something for this little boy. He is without hope."

This is the way Johnny Morris introduced us to the nine-year-old blind Mohdullah. Johnny, growing up as an orphan in Savannah, Georgia, felt real empathy for the Afghan boy.

He and I took Mohdullah to a doctor to have his eyes examined and learned he was incurably blind. Nothing medically could be done for him.

Johnny had taken a special interest in Mohdullah's future and was disappointed to learn that the Afghan Ministry of Education had no plans to teach the blind. All Mohdullah could look forward to was a mosque school where he would learn to memorize the Koran. Then he would be paid for reciting it at funerals, weddings, and other functions.

That prospect was not good enough for Johnny Morris. Having inherited a fortune from his parents, he was looking for a way to share it. So he made an offer to the Afghan Ministry of Education. For an entire year, he would pay all the expenses for a school for the blind—the building, furnishings, teachers' salaries—if the Ministry would agree to take over operating costs after that year.

The Afghan Cabinet members were impressed that a person from another country was concerned about their blind. However, they felt they could not spare teachers or money for a school for the blind. The reason? Many sighted children in the country still did not have an opportunity for schooling.

Before Johnny Morris left Afghanistan, he bought Mohdullah a flute, and left a small scholarship for his support. Johnny did not want the money to be given outright to him, but wanted him to earn it by doing odd jobs. Each week Mohdullah came to the church, with his smaller sighted sister leading him, and pulled dandelions and weeds from the lawn of the church garden. It was easy for him to feel the difference between the choking weeds and blades of grass.

About this time we had a visit from Dr. Isobel Grant, from Los Angeles, California, who herself was completely blind. She had her Ph.D. from Oxford University and was working under a Fulbright Grant. She was traveling to various countries to help with the education of the blind. She encouraged my wife Betty to teach Mohdullah to read and write Dari Braille.

Betty agreed, thinking the lessons would only take a couple of hours a week. Little did she realize that teaching the blind would soon be her full-time occupation.

When the lessons began, Mohdullah told Betty about two other blind friends who wanted to "read with their fingers." The three boys soon went through the whole first reader of the Afghan educational system. The primer had been typed in Dari Braille by Hans Werner, a Christian construction worker from Germany, who had been trained in the education of the blind in one of Pastor Christoffel's schools in Isfahan, Iran, and helped in his spare time.

Then in November 1965 the prayers of Johnny Morris and many others were finally answered. Dr. Mohammed Anas, the Afghan Minister of Education, accepted an invitation for tea at our home. first we showed him the movie *The Miracle Worker*, the story of Helen Keller. Then Dr. Anas met the three blind boys who had read to him from the first primer. He had never seen Braille read before, nor did he realize that there was a Dari system for it.

At first he thought the boys had memorized everything. But when he selected several parts of the book, he suddenly realized that the boys were reading.

"This is magic!" he exclaimed. In fact, he was so thrilled that he invited the blind boys, along with the Afghan girl who was helping, to come to his office at the Ministry the next day. There he gave them presents, offered the Afghan girl a scholarship to go abroad and study how to work with the blind. He also announced over the radio and in the newspapers that any blind person who wanted to learn Braille and handicrafts should come to our home. The advertising worked and it wasn't long before we were swamped with more than 75 blind students.

Betty had to give up her teaching at the Christian school, Ahlman Academy, in order to meet this new opportunity. Several church members volunteered to help out, and another outreach of the Kabul Community Christian church was under way. Pastor Sigfried Wiesinger, the director of the Christoffel Mission to the Blind in Germany, was invited to come by Monika Harper, who was now helping Betty. He gave us much needed advice. His assistance was invaluable in those first hectic months.

We had been in Afghanistan for fifteen years as tentmakers, and there were no missionaries there at the time. When we learned that some of these blind could see again if they had cataract operations, we asked the government for permission to bring in doctors and nurses. They agreed, aware they would be missionaries.

We called it the International Afghan Mission, for Christ's Name: "I AM." In John 8:12, Jesus says, "I AM the light of the world." In the Afghan Dari language, "light" is *noor*. So we called the program N.O.O.R., or National Organization for Ophthalmic Rehabilitation.

We rented property for the new school, next door to where the church was meeting, and the school was dedicated with the name, the Blind Institute of Noor in Afghanistan (BINA), which in Dari means "sight."

Skilled teachers of the blind came from abroad, including the United States, Finland, the Netherlands, and Germany. Then local Afghans were trained.

Eventually, the first six years of the Afghan Ministry of Education curriculum were offered in Dari Braille. Handicrafts also were taught, as well as English. Students who wanted to continue their education could attend sighted schools. Those who preferred to continue with handicrafts did so in their homes.

At first the pupils where all boys, but after several years blind girls and tiny children started coming as well.

Soon the rented house next door was overflowing, and we decided to build a school on the same property planned for Kabul's new Eye Institute. Oxford Famine Relief (OXFAM), a British Relief agency, gave money for the construction.

Dr. Howard Harper, an ophthalmologist from New Zealand headed up the building of both the NOOR Eye Hospital and the Institute for the Blind. The Church in Germany gave the funds for the hospital.

As the blind Afghans began receiving Christ as their Savior, the persecution started. By then we had two Institutes for the Blind in Afghanistan, the one in Kabul with more than 100 students and another in Herat, 700 miles to the west with more than 40 blind.

Then in March 1973 the unthinkable happened. The reactionary Muslim government under Prime Minister Musa Shafiq closed down the Blind Institutes because some of the blind had become Christians. Foreign teachers were ordered to leave Afghanistan within one week, and some students went back to begging on the streets.

However, our great disappointment turned to joy. In 1979 the Communist régime reopened the school for the blind under the direction of a former BINA graduate.

This was the fulfillment of the promise the Lord had given us in 1973: "And I will lead the blind by a way they do not know, in paths they do not know I will guide them. I will make darkness into light before them and rugged places into plains. These are the things I will do, and I will not forsake them" (Isaiah 42:16).

Silkworms, Trout, and Ducklings—
Gifts from a Chinese Agricultural Genius

We had a talented Chinese elder in our church in Kabul, Afghanistan, by the name of Dr. Kinston Keh *(for the story on his wife, see "The Futility of Ancestor Worship" in Chapter 3)*. Before the first World War, he left China to go to France, where he studied agriculture. Later he returned to China and became president of a silk manufacturing company. He was known as an expert in silk production as well as a genius in agriculture.

While he was in China, Dr. Keh had Chou En-lai as one of his students, whom he sent to France for further studies. It was while Chou En-lai was in France that he became a Communist. Dr. Keh was greatly saddened by this.

Even before Dr. Keh himself accepted Christ, his mother had become a Christian. She had taken ill and had gone to a Christian hospital, where they treated her very well. Sensing a different spirit there, she asked them what it was.

"It is the Spirit of Jesus Christ," they told her. "We believe He's alive, and we're serving people in His Name. As He healed people, we also are healing people."

This so moved Dr. Keh's mother that she accepted Christ as her Savior in that hospital. When she came home, she wanted to be baptized.

"If you're baptized," her husband told her, "you will disgrace our family, and I will leave home."

"I love you as my husband and I love my family," she answered, "but Jesus Christ is God and the Bible says we should be baptized. Whatever you do is up to you, but I must obey God." So she followed through with her plans for baptism.

Her husband then left home.

Since Dr. Keh was the oldest son, his mother asked him to attend her baptism.

"My father has refused to go, so I cannot go," he told his mother.

Nevertheless, his mother went and was baptized.

Later on her husband came back home. Then he accepted the Lord and became an even stronger Christian than his wife!

Years later Dr. Keh himself became a Christian and was baptized in China. He regretted that he had not attended his mother's baptism and wanted to make amends.

At the time of the Communist takeover, Dr. Keh was the president of the largest silk producing company in China, making him a capitalist and a prime target for the Communists. So they tried to kill him.

Forced to flee for his life, Dr. Keh came to Afghanistan with the United Nations to head up the silk industry for that country.

He did a marvelous job. Whereas the Afghans had been importing silkworm eggs from France and Russia, Dr. Keh crossed eggs from China and Japan to produce a hybrid silkworm that generated double and triple the amount of silk. Whereas the Russian and French cocoons only produced 500 meters of silk, Dr. Keh's hybrid cocoons produced 1200 to 1500 meters.

To get his hybrids, Dr. Keh waited for the eggs to hatch and the worms to grow and make cocoons. Before the moths emerged, he determined the sex of each one. Then he would place a Chinese male moth with a Japanese female moth, and vice versa.

In addition, Dr. Keh brought mulberry trees from Japan that would grow fifteen feet in one year. They could be cut just like cabbages, without having to climb the trees to cut the leaves. He had workers just cut off the branches and place them over the silkworms, who would climb onto the branches and eat the leaves.

The next year, the tree would grow fifteen feet again, and the entire process would be repeated.

Silkworm eggs take a year to hatch. As a scientist, Dr. Keh knew how to boil these eggs in sulfuric acid for a certain number of seconds, enabling them to hatch in three weeks instead!

Dr. Keh introduced this scientific silk production to the farmers in Afghanistan who were growing poppies for opium. The farmers made more money from silk than from opium.

So Dr. Keh not only replaced the opium industry with silk production—but he also developed Afghanistan's weaving and silk exporting industry!

Yet when he looked around and saw the great needs of the people, he searched for ways to help them even more.

He came to me one time and said, "You know, the poor people in this country need better fish to eat. We must try to do something." The fish in the lakes and streams were what we call trash fish. They were a type of carp with lots of bones in them, and the meat tasted like mud.

So I wrote to the Church back in Schenectady, New York, and an elder there got in touch with the New York State Department of Conservation.

"Our *minister extra-muros* (outside-the-walls) is interested in getting rainbow trout eggs for Afghanistan," he wrote.

When they heard *minister extra-muros*, they thought my first name was "Extra" and my last name was "Muros"! They wrote back saying, "We're happy to hear that Rev. Muros is interested in getting trout eggs for Afghanistan."

In the meantime, Dr. Keh and I traveled around Afghanistan and caught fish in the lakes and streams. I learned how to throw the net just like the disciples Peter, Andrew, James, and John would cast them into the Sea of Galilee. In one throw I caught thirty-three fish! Dr. Keh studied them to make sure that the trout would be compatible with the local fish and not just be food for them. It turned out that the local fish were vegetarian.

We received 25,000 eggs from the New York State Department of Conservation. They were flown to Afghanistan in three days. Dr. Keh had built a hatchery with fresh water flowing through it, and we placed the eggs there.

We lost the first shipment because of an unexpected freeze which turned the water into ice. But Dr. Keh was able to get another order of trout eggs from Japan.

The trout eggs hatched, and he fed beef liver to the fish since liver was cheap in Afghanistan. As a result, the fish grew very quickly into fingerlings. Then we stocked them in the streams and lakes of Afghanistan. Because the local trash fish were bony and vegetarian, the trout ate them up and grew very fast in the wild as well.

One time the King of Afghanistan and one of his princes were fishing in a mountain stream, and the prince hooked one of these rainbow trout. It gave him a great fight. When he finally landed it on the banks of the stream, he and the King cooked it right on the spot. To their amazement, all the bones came out with the backbone. When they tasted it, it was so delicious that the King ordered the Ministry of Agriculture to expand the project.

The government built a large hatchery. What the church had done on a small scale, the government did on a much grander scale, stocking trout and other fish all over the country. Then the King said to Dr. Keh:

"We're very grateful that you have introduced these fish into Afghanistan. Could you possibly get some Long Island ducklings as well?"

Many people don't realize that missionaries brought the Peking Duck from China to our West Coast. From there, it developed into the well-known Long Island duckling industry.

I wrote to Christians in a church in Long Island, asking them if they could buy us forty-eight Long Island Duckling eggs and send them by air to Afghanistan. And they did!

It took eighteen days for the eggs to be shipped by air from the States through Pakistan that summer, where temperatures reached 120 degrees in the shade! When the eggs arrived, Dr. Keh said, "I'm afraid they're all cooked from the heat. But let's pray. If God could give us one pair, that's all we need." So we prayed.

Then we put the duck eggs under some hens that were setting. Now, it takes twenty-one days to hatch a hen's egg, but twenty-eight days to hatch a duck egg. Yet the hens didn't seems to mind and they sat on these eggs for an extra week!

Of the forty-eight eggs, only three hatched. Two were drakes and one was a female duck.

You should have seen the mother hen who thought these were her chicks. She would march them around the yard. When the little ducklings came to water, they would dive right in and swim around, while the mother hen would stay at the edge just having a fit. The ducks, however, didn't pay any attention to her. This reminded me of Jesus' lament: "Oh Jerusalem, Jerusalem, how often I wanted to gather your children together, as a hen gathers her chicks under her wings, but you were not willing."

After these ducklings grew big enough, we presented them to the King. That one female laid more than eighty eggs the first season. The King was so thrilled that he autographed and numbered each egg so that no one could steal or eat any of them. Now these ducks are all over Afghanistan.

The ducks were cheaper to raise than chickens because they fed in the irrigation ditches. I once saw a poor man carrying two of these beautiful big white birds under his arms to sell. The Afghans not only ate the meat for nutrition, but they also used the feathers for quilts and down-filled clothes. At those high altitudes, it gets cold!

Although we did not recognize it at the time, God did something else through those ducks. The ducks protected the sheep against parasites. And sheep herding is the chief form of livelihood in Afghanistan. Afghanistan's 40 million sheep provided that country's main industry—wool for everything from coats and hats to carpets and cloth.

Sheep are vulnerable to liver fluke, a parasitic disease transmitted through a slug. The eggs then attach themselves to the grass or get into the water, which the sheep drink, and then get inside the liver, eventually killing the sheep. When the sheep die, the parasites are released into the grass, and the cycle begins all over again.

The ducks loved eating those slugs! And in that way, the ducks broke the vicious cycle of the liver fluke.

Several years after all this took place, my wife and I were out driving in Afghanistan one summer and we saw snow!

"How can there be snow here in summer?" I wondered.

When we came closer, we saw that the ground was covered with hundreds of these beautiful white ducks.

Persecuted for the Sake of the Gospel

Wherever the Gospel is taken, you will have opposition. Satan will attack, and the evil powers that control those areas will incite people to persecute Christians. The Apostle Paul wrote, "Those who live godly lives in Christ Jesus will suffer persecution."

A businessman for the Lord

In 1946, a Christian businessman, Dennis Clark, imported bicycles from the West into Afghanistan and exported Afghan nuts, fruit, and karakul sheepskin. He was only able to stay in Afghanistan two weeks.

Even in that short period of time, he said, he could sense the power of evil because it was so great. It seemed as if a dark cloud were hovering over Afghanistan all the time. He would try to pray but couldn't. His prayers just didn't seem to get through because of the power of Satan in that country. At that time, there was not a single Christian in the whole nation.

One day the secret police sent a student to his hotel room to ask him how he could become a Christian. Dennis Clark thought that this was the opportunity he had been praying for, for years. So he shared the Gospel with the student. But it was a trap.

When the government heard what he had done, they forced him to leave Afghanistan, under guard, all the way to the border at the Khyber pass. There they told him, "Don't ever come back again."

He baptized an American in Saudi Arabia

A classmate of mine in seminary, the Rev. Bill Antablin, was pastoring internationals in Saudi Arabia. Among them was an American who became a Christian and asked to be baptized. When the Saudi Government discovered that Bill had done this, they ordered him to leave the country.

"But he is not a Saudi Arabian," my classmate protested in Arabic. "He's an American."

"It doesn't matter," the authorities told him. "No one is allowed to baptize anyone in Saudi Arabia!"

In similar manner, during the Gulf War, none of the American chaplains were allowed to wear a cross on their uniform. However, a former student of mine, who was a chaplain with the troops there, was able to baptize 31 soldiers in one service. The Muslim government in Saudi Arabia was not able to prevent this.

No Christian can pray here

In 1989 Dr. Robert Cooley, president of Gordon-Conwell, arranged for all the faculty to go to the Holy Land for two weeks.

Professor Jack Davis was with us in the Dome-Of-The-Rock mosque, which is built on the platform where the Temple once stood.

So deeply moved was he to be there, that he began to pray silently to himself. He had bowed his head when a Muslim guard stopped him immediately.

"You are not allowed to pray here," he told him. "Only Muslims are allowed to pray here!"

I mention all this for one reason: to prepare you for what is to come. Remember, wherever the Gospel is preached, you will have opposition, always.

Accused of Spying in the Holy Land

When our children were old enough to appreciate the Holy Land, we spent some time there as a family. We would read the Bible together in the morning before visiting the historic sites. Then, at each place we visited, we would stop and read in the Scriptures what had taken place there.

For example, we did this in the Garden of Gethsemane as we sat under the olive trees there and read the passages which dealt with this place.

I borrowed this idea from Dawson Trotman, who started the Navigators. He told me he had taken his Bible to the Holy Land and had done this.

Once we went to the Sea of Galilee where we swam and caught fish. In the Sea of Galilee there are fish called St. Peter's fish with flat mouths.

When Christ told Peter to go throw a hook into the Sea and the first fish he caught would have enough money for both their taxes, Peter caught one of these flat-mouthed fish!

Apparently, someone getting out of the boat must have dropped a coin into the sea. Seeing it shining in the water, a fish must have grabbed it and was probably trying to swallow it when it saw Peter's hook. When it swallowed the hook, Peter pulled it in and found the money in its mouth!

These flat-mouthed fish still swim in the Sea of Galilee, and we caught some and ate them. Our children will never forget that experience.

We also went to the top of the Mount of Olives. Although the Muslims don't believe Jesus died on the cross, they believe He ascended to heaven. There is a mosque built on the place where they think He actually ascended. From the roof of that mosque, using my movie camera, I took pictures of Jerusalem as it lay below after first getting permission from the guide. Then I ended with an upward scan to the top of the minaret, against the sky where our Lord had ascended into heaven.

When I scanned the top of the minaret, I saw a Jordanian soldier with huge field glasses spying on Israel. This was 1964 and Jordan still held the area of Jerusalem where you find the Mount of Olives and the Temple Mount.

One of the soldiers saw that I had captured this on film.

"You weren't allowed to take that picture!" he said.

"Well, I asked if it would be all right and the guide said yes."

"No, you can't have that picture! You must pull all your film out of the camera!" the soldier ordered.

Now, that roll of film had all the pictures from our trip, and I did not want to give it up.

"Could I see your commanding officer?" I asked. So they brought me to him. When I tried to explain things to him, he burst out:

"No," the officer said. "You can't have those pictures!"

So they pulled the entire roll of film out of the camera.

The Jordanians knew they were not allowed to use mosques for military spying, that it broke the terms of their agreement with Israel. So they were afraid the film would expose what they were doing. But I was the one they accused of spying.

Despite this, our children will never forget the vivid scenes as we read the Bible together at each historic site. Our Holy Land visit set Scripture scenes within the frames of our memory.

The "Fully" Inspired Word

When we were starting the International Afghan Mission in the summer of 1965, there were ten missions working on the border of Afghanistan, waiting for the chance to enter. We could see the time coming when Afghanistan would allow medical doctors and nurses into the country.

At that time, however, all of us in Afghanistan were tentmakers or self-supporting missionaries. We had taken secular jobs but our purpose was to witness for Christ. And rather than have these ten missions come in at cross purposes, we invited all of them to send representatives to a conference to be held in the mountains of Murree, Pakistan.

We spent the first day in prayer and then considered the matter of coming in together as an evangelical fellowship. We used the constitution of the United Mission of Nepal as our basic document from which to work. And there in the basis of faith, it stated that every missionary coming into the country accepted the Scriptures—the canonical books of the Old and New Testaments—as the "inspired Word of God."

Among our group, some felt that this was not strong enough and suggested that we add the word "infallible" so that it would read, "the inspired, infallible Word of God." Well, this caused a split right down the middle.

Dr. Norval Christy, a graduate of Harvard Medical School and a Presbyterian missionary in Pakistan, spoke up:

"I believe God has called me to work in Afghanistan," he said. "But if I were to approve adding this word 'infallible,' I'm afraid my mission board would not allow me to go—thinking this was a separatist and fundamentalist group. Even though I believe in the infallibility of Scripture, if I were to vote for this word, it would prevent me from serving in Afghanistan."

Bishop Woolmer, who had been President of the InterVarsity Chapter at Oxford, and who was now a missionary with the Church Missionary Society in Lahore, Pakistan, had a suggestion. "Could we find a word that meant the same thing but was both Scriptural and positive?"

"The word 'infallible' does not appear in the Bible and it is negative," he said.

"No, it must be included," said Jack Ringer, who used to be a Cold Stream Guard in the British Army. Before coming to Christ, he was in charge of gambling for his whole regiment. "Either 'infallible' is put in there or we won't join the International Afghan Mission."

We decided to meet six months later. All were to consult with their missions headquarters to try to find some way of breaking this impasse. Before the next meeting, I read a number of confessions of faith, trying to find a suitable word. But I couldn't find one that was both biblical and positive.

In the winter of 1966, the group gathered again, this time in Kabul. Everything went well, but once more everyone was split over this word "infallible." On the final morning I arose early, opened my Bible and prayed.

"Lord, show me a word that is both biblical and positive. Don't let Your work in this land be hindered because of one word."

I came to II Timothy 3:16, which says: "All Scripture is given by inspiration of God." Then I thought of adding just one little word "fully" so that it read: "the canonical books of the Old and New Testament are the *fully* inspired Word of God."

At breakfast, Dr. Howard Harper of New Zealand, who was already working in Afghanistan as an ophthalmologist, was eating with Jack

Ringer. Jack poked him with his elbow and said, "Well, brother, you're getting in with a strange group of bedfellows."

Later that morning, when I suggested adding this one little word "fully," everyone bought it. They voted unanimously to accept the statement of faith and to start the International Afghan Mission!

That night, while we were on our knees offering prayers of thanksgiving, we heard someone start to snore. It was Jack Ringer. This time it was Dr. Harper who had to poke him to wake him up! Obviously, Jack was very relaxed and happy with the outcome.

"Jack," Dr. Harper said later, "this morning you said I was getting in bed with a strange group of bedfellows. By noon you had climbed in yourself, and by evening your were snoring!"

The Folly of Liberal Teachings

As a prep school student at the high school level, I was taught the higher criticism of the Bible. At first I believed these theories because I thought the teachers knew more about these things than I did.

Yet through my habit of reading the Bible each day—which my father encouraged—I realized that these critical views did not agree with the original Source.

When I began to investigate all the attacks on Scripture, I found that the Bible was right in every single case. So by investigation and by faith, I accepted the Scriptures as the infallible Word of God. Since then, I have turned to the Scriptures when anyone has come to me with a problem and have found the solution there each time.

If it is the Word of God and so is without error, we don't have to be afraid of investigation. It has been wonderful to see how God has honored His Word and shown it to be absolutely dependable.

In 1933, liberals published *Humanist Manifesto Number One*, which denied the existence of God. That was the heyday of liberalism, before the rise of Nazi Germany and World War II.

Professor John Dewey of Columbia University, the prophet of progressive education, signed this manifesto.

Progressive education has by and large had an evil effect on schooling in this country, based as it is on the false assumption that people are by nature good. It disregards the fact that humanity is sinful, since the fall. Students are therefore allowed to develop on their own.

When my parents were missionaries in Iran, we came back on furlough one year, and my younger brother and sister went to one of those progressive schools in New York City. One day, it started to rain, so my mother sent me to their school with their raincoats.

When I arrived, the class was in bedlam. I wondered why there was no teacher. Then in the back row, I saw the teacher, humbly sitting there, watching the class carry on. He was required to let them express themselves as they wished. They were to be allowed to bloom on their own, like flowers. No discipline of any kind was allowed. So much for "progressive" education, which has proved regressive as Biblical principles have been rejected.

Liberalism Affects Student Missions

The liberalism of the 1920's through the 1940's even affected the Student Missionary Conferences.

In 1944 I remember attending a Student Volunteer Movement quadrennial held at Wooster College in Wooster, Ohio. It had departed so far from its roots and foundation that when some of us joined together for a prayer meeting, one of the leaders broke it up.

"We don't want any emotionalism here," he said. He wouldn't let us pray! Imagine! Their liberal ideas and practices had become more important than the Bible and prayer.

Yet the Urbana Student Missionary Conference is really an extension of the Student Volunteer Movement (SVM) that was first organized more than 100 years ago, in 1886, under Dwight L. Moody in Mount Hermon, Massachusetts.

When the Student Volunteer Movement began, Dr. Adoniram Judson Gordon was one of its leaders, along with Dr. Arthur T. Pierson. It was Dr. Pierson who popularized the slogan: "The evangelization of the world in this generation." He believed that every generation is responsible for evangelizing its world.

The Student Volunteer Movement held the Scriptures in high esteem. That's why they went out to evangelize the world.

I had signed the SVM decision card that read: "God helping me, I purpose to be a foreign missionary." My parents had signed this card as well, and therefore went to Iran in 1919.

More than 100,000 people signed that statement. Of this number, more than 20,000 actually served in foreign lands!

Kathryn Kuhlman

On one of our furloughs to the United States, Betty and I were only going to be here for three months so I wanted to find out what was happening in the churches.

We went to Pittsburgh to one of Kathryn Kuhlman's services at the first Presbyterian Church. We were told to get there by 6:00 a.m. in order to be assured of seats at the 9:00 a.m. service. When we arrived, already the whole street was just packed with people waiting for the Church to open.

Finally the doors were opened at 8:00 a.m., and we just barely squeezed in before they closed them again.

The only seats available were near the choir. Yet I appreciated that because it was right behind Kathryn Kuhlman and we could see everything that was going on.

It was simply amazing. Kathryn Kuhlman gave Christ all the glory. She began the service by reading from the Scriptures, giving honor to Jesus. Then the Holy Spirit began to give her a word of knowledge for specific people whom the Lord had healed.

"There's a man up there in the balcony sitting in the second row," she said, "who has just been healed of lung cancer. Would you please come forward and testify." So this man came down to the front along with his pastor. His Lutheran pastor had driven all night from Reading, Pennsylvania, to bring him to that service.

"Isn't this wonderful," Kathryn Kuhlman said. "This pastor loves this member of his congregation so much that he has driven all night to bring this man here. The Lord has seen that and has now touched this man and healed him." The man was then touching his toes, which he hadn't been able to do for months because of the lung cancer.

Kathryn Kuhlman then prayed for him and he was slain in the Spirit. Now, many people ask if that's in the Bible. I think it is. The Apostle John tells us in Revelation 1:10 and 17 that he was in the Spirit on the Lord's Day and when Christ appeared to him in glory, he fell at His feet as though dead. I think this is also what happened when Jesus Christ was arrested. When they came to arrest him, our Lord asked whom they were seeking.

"Jesus of Nazareth," they said.

"I am He." In saying that, Christ took the name of Jehovah to Himself. He took the name which the Jews wouldn't even pronounce, the name of God revealed to Moses, which was "I AM.". We read that they all fell over backwards. Now, why did they fall? Because the power of God was there, and I believe they were slain in the Spirit.

Then during this Kathryn Kuhlman meeting, a second man came forward and said that he had been a alcoholic. He said he drank a case of whisky every week, and his family was ready to leave him. He was in California when he watched Kathryn Kuhlman on television. Then he knelt down in front of the TV set and asked Jesus to forgive him.

"You know," he said, "every cell in my body was reprogrammed. I haven't touched a drop of liquor since that time. My wife and I moved from California to Pittsburgh, where she has a job in the skyscraper just across the street from the church. I've tried to get a job here, but when they check my references they write back and say that I am a religious nut."

As long as he was an alcoholic, he was all right. But as soon as he accepted Christ, they thought he was a nut and wouldn't recommend him. Before his conversion, the only time he had been to church was when he was baptized as a baby and once when he went to a funeral.

That morning, while in his wife's office, he looked down and saw this crowd on the street. He asked what was happening, and was told it was a Kathryn Kuhlman meeting. "Since I'm not working, I came down," he said.

She then prayed for him that the Lord would find him a job, and he too was slain in the Spirit. The ushers had to grab him. Sometimes the power would be so strong that the ushers would keel over as well.

The healing service went from 9:00 a.m. to 1:00 in the afternoon. During that time, I slipped out to visit the senior pastor of the church, Dr. Robert Lamont, whom I knew.

"Bob, what do think of all this?" I asked him.

"Well," he replied, "Kathryn Kuhlman wanted to have a place to meet, but no one in Pittsburgh would allow her to use their facility. So I went to my session to ask them if we could let her use the Church. They said on one condition: that she would let me see all her accounts to be sure nothing was done that was dishonest.

"I told her this and she replied, 'By all means. I'll be happy to have you do that.' That first time she paid for using the church, but the session returned all the money to her.

"'The Church is meant to be used for services like this,' they told her. So Kathryn Kuhlman continues to use this church every Friday morning, and the place is packed out each time."

Years later I was invited to preach in that church. I stayed in the hotel next door and had a chance to talk with the maid who was taking care of my room. I found out she was a born-again Christian, so I asked her how she became one.

"Through Miss Kuhlman," she told me. "She used to stay here when she came for the healing services. We still have a Bible study and prayer meeting for hotel personnel, which began when she first came here."

I know there are all kinds of criticisms of her ministry. Yet Jesus said: "By their fruits you shall know them."

I'll give you an example of the prejudice against Kathryn Kuhlman. My wife Betty is a wonderful kindergarten teacher and has the gift of teaching. She was doing that in Canada before we met. When we came to the States after we had been forced to leave Afghanistan, she wanted to teach child evangelism because she had taken courses in it.

A woman came to interview her about this. She asked Betty several questions. One of them was, "Have you ever been to a Kathryn Kuhlman service?"

"Yes," Betty said, "I went to one."

"If that's the case, then we can't have you teaching child evangelism." Betty was rejected.

Yet, when we were at that one Kathryn Kuhlman service, it reminded us of the time when Jesus was healing people. A lady in front of us had a little child in her arms who was having fits and convulsions, even while the mother held her. Ambulances were driving up and people were being wheeled out into the lower part of the church.

Now, only about 10 percent were healed at these services.

"I don't know why the Lord doesn't heal more," Kathryn Kuhlman used to say. "But it's not I, but God who does it through me." She couldn't understand why the Lord didn't heal everybody.

Yet how wonderful that 10 percent of the people found healing!

John Wimber

While I was Dean of the Chapel at Gordon-Conwell, more than a hundred students in the Seminary signed a petition requesting that John Wimber be invited to speak on campus. At the time it did not seem wise because this was at the height of the controversy at Fuller Seminary over the Signs and Wonders Course which he and Peter Wagner were teaching.

In the summer of 1989, Betty and I went to a John Wimber conference on Long Island, since the Bible says to test the spirits whether they be of God (I John 4:1). It was held in a church which had formerly been a theater. There were 1600 seats and all of them were filled. In fact they had to cut off registrations early since they had no more room.

John Wimber came to Christ when he was 28, while he was playing the saxophone in a band, so he has a good appreciation for music. Thus a praise band led us in worship. Following the worship, John expounded the Scriptures on the subject of prophecy.

Then came a time of ministry. The Lord showed John Wimber, through words of knowledge, whom He wanted to heal. He said, "Would all those who can only see through one eye come forward. The Lord wants to heal your blind eye." Seven people came forward to stand before the platform. Then he said, "The Lord told me there would be eight. Where is the eighth?" I thought to myself, "He is certainly going out on a limb saying this." But a man then came down from the balcony and confessed that he too was blind in one eye.

John Wimber then asked people to gather around these eight and pray for them, since the Lord wanted to heal them. This impressed me that he was seeking to involve others and teach them how to minister, rather than trying to do it all himself. A lady then went to the microphone on the platform and said, "I was born blind. When the doctors operated on one eye, I regained vision in that eye. But I have never seen with my other eye until today. Now I can see through it as well for the first time in my life!"

As Betty and I saw and heard this, we recognized it as a real work of God. So I spoke to John Wimber about coming to speak at Gordon-Conwell sometime in the future.

We decided on July 1991 to coincide with the start of the annual Seminar on the Holy Spirit in World Evangelization sponsored by the Adoniram Judson Gordon School of World Missions.

However there were some who opposed this. They feared that trouble would erupt even as it had at Fuller Seminary. Finally, we reached a compromise. John would give an exposition at Gordon-Conwell for two days and then, on the third day, he would hold a practical demonstration of ministry, sponsored by the Vineyard churches in the area. The ministry session would take place at Endicott College nearby. John graciously complied with this.

On the third day, the 1200-seat capacity gym was packed. After a time of worship and Scripture exposition, the Lord worked in a demonstration of healing power.

John Wimber said there was a young woman who had trouble with both her arms. An illness was causing the arms to become deformed. He asked her to stand. He even said her name was Ruth. When she stood, he asked her to move into the aisle and requested people around her to pray for her. That afternoon I met her and asked her if she had been healed. She said "Yes!" And she extended her arms. They were perfectly normal. I then asked her if she believed in Jesus Christ as her Savior and Lord. She said, "I do now!"

John Wimber then asked all who had back trouble to stand because the Lord wanted to heal them. More than 150 stood up. Since there was not enough room in the gym for people to gather around and pray over each one, John asked that they move outdoors and pray there.

A Gordon-Conwell alumnus, the Rev. Leonard Cowan, now an Episcopal rector in the Northampton area, was sitting with his wife next to Betty and me. He said that he had terrible back trouble, and went out for prayer. Later I saw him and asked him how he was. He said that it was just as if the Lord had put a heating pad at the base of his spine, and the heat was still going down his right leg! He felt better than he had in years.

At the evening meeting, one of my former students, Greg Clark, who is co-pastoring a Vineyard church in the area, found Betty and me sitting at the back of the auditorium. He kindly invited us to sit in the front row, exchanging seats with him and his wife. When we accepted, they graciously sat on the floor. We were thus only a few feet away from John Wimber.

During the service John asked all of us to pray silently for the things we wanted God to do for us and through us. I prayed that the Lord would use me to reach Muslims with signs and wonders.

Then John Wimber asked couples to come forward who had never had children but wanted to have them. Around 30 couples came to the front. He said, "The Lord is going to give you children, and this is a token of the hundreds of thousands of spiritual children God is going to give Christians in New England." Since then two of these couples have told me they are expecting for the first time.

After the meeting, I wanted to thank John Wimber personally for taking the time and trouble to come, but he was already gone. I spoke to Bob Branch, another Vineyard pastor, who would be taking him to the airport and asked him to express my gratitude. He told me that John Wimber was up on the platform behind the curtain praying with a couple and that Betty and I could see him there. I did get to thank him.

Then John said to me, "Christy, while you were praying, the Lord showed me that you were asking Him to work through you with signs and wonders among the Muslims. He wants you to know that He is going to do this through you!"

To me this was the climax of the whole seminar!

Worshiping As One People

When my father was a missionary pastor of the church in Tabriz, Iran, he was thrilled that the church included converts from among Muslims, Jews, Armenian Apostolics, Nestorians, and even Zoroastrians or sun-worshipers. These people, who had been massacring each other, were now worshiping and taking communion together. That was in the 1920's.

When my wife and I were forced to leave Afghanistan in 1973, we spent a little over a year in Tehran. This was about fifty years after my parents' time.

A very interesting thing had happened there.

Christian converts from other religious backgrounds, like the people in the church my father had pastored, had come and settled in Tehran. By 1973, Tehran had more than five million people.

After they arrived in the capital, they worshiped as homogeneous units. This was natural. They were all members of the same denomination: the Presbyterian Church. So there was an Armenian Presbyterian Church, a Nestorian Presbyterian Church, a Messianic Jewish Presbyterian Church, even a Presbyterian Church made up of Muslim converts.

Years later, I received a phone call from Dr. Russell Rosser, the pastor of the First Baptist Church in Flushing, New York.

"We have more than 500 Afghan refugees who have settled right in our church neighborhood," he said. "We don't know how to reach them. Do you have any suggestions?"

"Their greatest holiday is New Year's on March 21," I said. "I would suggest you invite them to the church on their New Year's Day, and have them bring their favorite foods for a pot-luck supper. Then you can have a special program. They'll love it!"

"Great," the pastor said. "Will you come?"

I went. Many Afghans came to this church and brought their specialities. The young people's choir in the church had learned songs in Dari, the Afghan language. This thrilled the Afghans because they had never heard Christians sing in church before. Islam regards music as sinful, so there is no music in their services.

But here in the church, they loved the music! So as the young people sang these songs in Dari, the Afghans were clapping away. They were so happy.

Then a Muslim convert from Iran give a wonderful testimony. He did it very cleverly.

"Once there was a young man in Iran," he began. Then he told the story of how "this young man" found Christ as his Savior, and how his sins had been forgiven, how he had joy in his heart for the first time, and that his life had new meaning. Then he ended with these words: "That young man was yours truly." How the Afghans clapped and clapped. That was Saturday night.

On Sunday morning, I was amazed to see six different congregations under one roof! They had a Chinese congregation with a pastor speaking in Mandarin. I preached to them through an interpreter. Practically every week they were baptizing new believers from mainland China! Then I went to a congregation of Russian refugees who were having a great revival ... then to a Portuguese congregation ... to a Jewish congregation ... and lastly to a Spanish one!

Finally there was an English service at 11:00 a.m. that welcomed everybody. All the children and young people of the other congregations attended this one because they knew English.

What a wonderful example of the homogeneous unit principle at work—and all under one church roof!

An Antique Gun

The old Afghan muzzleloaders used in the 1800's to fight the British are a real curiosity, with their extra long barrels.

While Dr. Herbert Mekeel, of the First Presbyterian Church in Schenectady, New York, was visiting with us in Afghanistan, he saw one of these and wanted it for his office back in the States. So before I left the country, I purchased one for him.

The only way I could fit the gun into my suitcase was to have the barrel sawed in half and store it corner-to-corner, along with the old lock-and-stock.

When my wife and I landed in Russian Central Asia, we had to indicate whether we were carrying any drugs or firearms.

So they would not think I was trying to cover anything up I wrote down "one antique gun."

Now the Russian customs officials didn't know what "antique" meant. One look at the word "gun," and they all came running. They knew we were on our way to the May Day Celebration in Moscow, and figured I would use this high-powered American rifle to shoot some of their leaders.

As they all gathered around my suitcase, I snapped open the lid. There lay the battered antique gun, its barrel sawed in half!

They all roared with laughter! And we had no more trouble.

The Prophecy

During the summer of 1990 I attended the "Congress on The Holy Spirit and World Evangelization" in Indianapolis. A man with the gift of prophecy, Paul Cain, was a speaker there.

I had never met him before.

While I was there, Betty and I received a letter of invitation to go to Afghanistan. It had been hand-carried by a doctor and his wife who had just returned from Kabul.

"Lord, what is Your will?" I had been praying.

Well, I went to a session where Paul Cain was speaking. Suddenly he stopped short and pointed directly at me, saying:

"Christy Wilson, God is going to take you back to Afghanistan, and you will be accepted by the people who once rejected you."

That prophecy was fulfilled in the spring of 1991 when we returned to Kabul for 23 days to work and pray with Christians.

Three Types of Speaking in Tongues

Many Christians do not understand that the Bible reveals three different forms of speaking in tongues.

First, you can speak in a foreign language unknown to you, but understood by someone else. Second, you can speak in a language known only to God, with the Holy Spirit giving the interpretation. Third, you can speak in a private prayer language with God alone.

A recognized foreign language

In Acts chapter 2, we have the many different languages which the Holy Spirit gave miraculously to the people gathered in Jerusalem on the Day of Pentecost. They had come from many countries but they heard, in their own language, praise to God for His wonderful works.

In Holland, in 1987, my wife and I met an Afghan who had come to Christ. Not knowing any other Afghan Christians, he thought he was the only one in the whole world. He visited a church in a tiny fishing village in Holland, a Pentecostal congregation where they spoke in tongues.

The Afghan thought this speaking in tongues was strange. Until one day ...

At that service, an elderly Dutch lady—who had never even set foot in Amsterdam let alone outside the country—spoke in his language, which was Afghan Dari!

"The Lord Jesus Christ is coming! The Lord Jesus Christ is coming!" she repeated in his dialect.

When he heard her speak, he knew this was a miracle from God. From then on he had no trouble accepting the speaking in tongues.

Another Afghan Christian I knew, a student, attended a church service while he was visiting in California. During that service, the pastor gave a message in tongues. After the service the Afghan went up to speak to the pastor.

"When were you in Afghanistan?" he asked.

"I've never been out of the United States," the pastor replied. "What do you mean?"

"You were talking in Pashtu, my mother tongue," said the Afghan. "You told how Jesus died for my sins and how He rose again from the dead."

"That was the Holy Spirit speaking to you through me," said the pastor. "I have never been to Afghanistan."

The Afghan student recognized this as a miracle. As a result, he has accepted the Lord.

This type of tongues-speaking is rare yet it still happens today on certain occasions.

Interpretation given by the Holy Spirit

There is a second kind of tongues mentioned in II Corinthians 14. Paul says that when someone gives a message in tongues during a service, it must be interpreted. Then only two or three should be given so that the service doesn't get out of hand. This is another way that the Lord gives us messages.

During a time when my wife and I were being persecuted in Afghanistan, we came back to the States on a home leave. Even the American Ambassador told us he was going to do everything in his power to prevent us from returning to Afghanistan.

We went to a Presbyterian church for a Saturday night service. No one knew us there. Someone gave a message in tongues, and another interpreted it. And the message was just for Betty and me.

"Don't be afraid to go back, because I am going with you. And do not be afraid of those who are persecuting you because I am going to confound them, and I am going to give the victory for the Lord's people."

We had planned to leave for Afghanistan in two days. It was such a wonderful blessing to receive this word of encouragement from the Lord. When we got back to Kabul, this Ambassador was dismissed from his post. God's message to us was fulfilled.

This is the second kind of tongues, and is more common.

Our prayer language with God

The third kind of tongues is also described in II Corinthians 14 and Romans 8:26. The latter states, "The Spirit Himself intercedes for us with groans that words cannot express." It is a private prayer language. I think that's what Christ prayed when He was in the garden. It says he cried out with strong cries. When you cry out in prayer, the Holy Spirit interprets the real meaning of those sounds or groans.

This type of speaking in tongues is the most common of all. And it brings about a new spiritual power in prayer. The first and second types are special gifts of the Holy Spirit, but all Christians can participate in this third type for communion with the Lord.

"Are You Willing to Die For Me?"

When World War II ended, I became Missionary Secretary for InterVarsity and visited campuses throughout North America.

Let me share an experience I had. As Dr. Addison Leitch, former Dean of the Faculty at Gordon-Conwell, said, "Don't apologize for personal experiences because they are the only kind we have."

While traveling in western Canada in March 1946, I visited Prairie Bible Institute in Alberta. There I told students how this was the greatest opportunity in history to evangelize the world. The war was over, China was open, and other countries were now accessible.

"Before the Lord chose His disciples, He prayed all night," I told them. "Where are these all-night prayer meetings now?"

But even as I spoke, the Holy Spirit convicted me of being a hypocrite since I had never spent a night in prayer. And here I was preaching beyond my depth.

Consequently, I decided to pray all night. Now, it's one thing to decide to spend the night in prayer, but it's another thing to know what to pray for during that time.

I had just finished reading a book by Robert Wilder, whom God used to start the Student Volunteer Movement. In this he had noted that the Bible study that meant the most to him was examining the Person and work of the Holy Spirit in Scripture. So I decided that I would take my concordance and study the Person and work of the Holy Spirit for half-an-hour from the Bible, and then pray for half-an-hour, and continue doing this throughout the night.

Towards morning, while I was praying and asking the Lord what He wanted me to do, I sensed the Lord speaking to me. I didn't hear an audible voice, but the Lord impressed this thought on my mind.

"Are you willing to do anything for me?"
"Yes, Lord," I answered. "I'm willing to do anything for You."
Then the Lord's voice came once more.
"Are you willing to die for Me?"
"Lord," I whispered, "You died for me, so I'll gladly die for Thee." And as I prayed that, something totally unexpected happened. The Holy Spirit fell on me in power.
The next morning when I spoke in chapel, the Lord worked in a new way. Many students volunteered for missions. The fruit of the Spirit—love, joy, peace, longsuffering, gentleness, goodness, faith, meekness, temperance—seemed to be multiplied many-fold.

The Billy Graham Telephone Ministry

More people pray to receive Christ over the telephones, while watching Billy Graham on television, than they do at the actual crusades. This whole idea of evangelism by phone was started by a missionary on furlough.

Dr. Hubert Mitchell, in the 1930's, had been evangelizing an unreached people group in the jungles of the Island of Sumatra in Indonesia. When he was in the States on furlough, he phoned a friend only to find he was not at home. So he left a message with the person who had answered. Then before hanging up, he felt led to ask, "Have you ever received Jesus Christ as your personal Savior?" The person said that he hadn't. Dr. Mitchell asked if he would like to. The man answered, "Yes." So he led him to the Lord on the phone.

This started the whole ministry of evangelism by phone which is being used so effectively by organizations like Campus Crusade, the Christian Broadcasting Network, and the Billy Graham Evangelistic Crusade. Dr. Mitchell has written about this in his book, *Putting Your Faith On The Line*, produced by Here's Life Publications.

A pastor in Minneapolis suggested that, along with the telecasts of the Graham Crusades, they also flash a telephone number on the screen which people could call for spiritual help. The first time they tried it, the phones were overloaded as tens of thousands of people tried to call.

There are now ten telephone centers, which stretch from Bermuda to Hawaii, which take calls during the four weeks a year when the crusades are televised.

Since we have one of these telephone centers in the Boston area, I have made it a requirement for my students in Personal Evangelism to participate. It has not only helped them learn how to lead people to Christ, but it has transformed their whole ministry. One student was reluctant to do it at first, but he took 23 calls in one night and led 11 people to Christ! These callers then receive the same follow-up materials given to the people who make decisions at the crusades. One of my women students said that it was just as if Billy Graham hooked a fish and then gave her the rod and reel to pull it in.

Once when I was home on furlough from Afghanistan in 1969, I attended the North American Congress on Evangelism which was headed up by Billy Graham and was held in Minneapolis. Dr. James Kennedy, who started Evangelism Explosion, was there. He led a pastors' seminar on personal evangelism which I attended. There were more than 600 pastors who took it.

Dr. Kennedy asked how many of them had taken a course in seminary, a Christian college or a Bible school where they were taught how to lead a person to Christ. Only three hands went up, or less than two per cent. He said that our Christian educational institutions were teaching very good things, but they were leaving out what was most important. He added that when our Lord started His seminary, He told His disciples, "Follow Me and I will make you fishers of men" (Matthew 4:19).

When I heard this, I determined that if I ever taught in a seminary, I would teach a course on personal evangelism. During my years at seminary, I never had a course on how to lead people to Christ. I learned it by watching a Christian businessman. He taught a Bible class at Princeton University, and then led students to Jesus Christ after the hour ended.

So when I was invited to teach at Gordon-Conwell, I started a course on personal evangelism. Even though it has been an elective, hundreds of students have taken it. One pastor around fifty years of age enrolled. Although he had graduated from an evangelical seminary, he had never led anyone to Christ. During the course he led five of his congregation to a saving knowledge of the Savior! He was so happy, he was "on cloud nine."

Dr. Adoniram Judson Gordon, who started the Boston Missionary Training Institute—which has now become Gordon College and Gordon-Conwell Theological Seminary—used to have the people in his church enter into a covenant. It stated:

> *We do solemnly covenant with each other that ... we will not forsake the assembling of ourselves together, or omit the great duty of prayer both for ourselves and for others ... that we will strive together for the support of a faithful evangelical ministry among us; that we will endeavor, by example and effort, to win souls to Christ.*

It is my prayer that the schools which bear his name, Gordon College and Gordon-Conwell Theological Seminary, will actively continue to promote the training and practice of personal evangelism.

An Evening With Billy and Ruth Graham

When I was invited to give the Staley Lectures on missions at Montreat-Anderson College in North Carolina, Ruth Graham attended them regularly. The Grahams live nearby, and Ruth does much to encourage the students, especially in missions.

One evening I was invited to the Grahams' home along with a Gordon-Conwell alumnus and his wife, Sam and Linda McGinn. We had a delightful time together. The "laughing fire" which Ruth has described in her book was burning in the large fireplace.

Ruth asked me to repeat the following story to Billy which I had told in one of the lectures. Billy liked it, and later used it as an illustration in one of his messages.

One time I was on an airplane in Afghanistan, preparing for departure. The door was shut, our seat belts were fastened, and we thought we were ready for take-off. Suddenly, through the window, I saw a man running toward the plane. I thought he must be one of the passengers who was late, and wondered whether they would let him on. Sure enough, he started pounding on the door of the plane.

The flight attendant looked at his watch. It was time for us to leave, so he was not about to open the door. But the man kept pounding louder and louder. Finally the flight attendant went back and opened the door a crack to see who it was. There, to everyone's amazement, stood the pilot!

We had locked the pilot out of the plane!

The ramp had already been pulled away, so they had to grab him by the elbows and hoist him up into the plane. As the pilot walked up the aisle, the Afghans—who have a good sense of humor—roared with laughter. He then got into the cockpit and we took off.

When this happened, I thought how much our lives are like this. We think we are in the right place and are all set to take off for heaven. But the question is, "Have we left the Pilot out?"

Jesus said, "Behold, I stand at the door and knock. If anyone hears My voice and opens the door, I will come in." He not only comes in to save us from our sins, but He has the flight plan for our lives which guides our ministry and ultimately takes us to heaven.

The Way Out

Shortly after Afghanistan opened its doors to tourists for the first time in 1957, as many as 100,000 people a year were visiting the country. Thousands of Western young people roamed the streets of Kabul and other cities.

Kabul was one of the meccas on the "Hippie Trail"—the route that Western youths traveled as they experimented with drugs and delved into Eastern religions. This was a romantic route that extended from Europe through Turkey, Iran, Afghanistan, Pakistan, and India to Nepal—and then back.

The local Afghans were stunned by the hordes of hippies who descended on their country, anxious to get the hard drugs produced from opium poppies, an indigenous Afghan crop. Hundreds were caught trying to smuggle drugs out of the country, and soon Afghan prisons were overflowing with foreigners. Many young people died of overdoses. Others lost their minds. Many of the women would engage in prostitution in order to satisfy their drug habits.

Desperate and disillusioned, some of these young people began seeking a further meaning in life.

We at the Kabul Community Christian Church sensed a wide open opportunity to help these young people get their lives back together again. And so began a saga that ended with one of the most unusual ministries I've ever had the privilege to be a part of.

First, members of our church contacted the Salvation Army headquarters about establishing a center in Kabul to care for these young people. They expressed an interest, but Afghan officials would not allow people wearing the Salvation Army uniform to work in their nation, since they would look like a foreign military force.

We also wrote to David Wilkerson of Teen Challenge, but this organization was already overextended and did not feel it could expand its ministry to Afghanistan.

Then one day Jim Cameron, of New Zealand, came through Kabul and told our church about Youth With A Mission (YWAM), an organization committed to training young people for evangelism. YWAM was eager to accept this challenge, and in July 1970 YWAM staff members Jim and Jan Rogers arrived in Kabul with seven dedicated young people. They stayed in the Nooristan Hotel, a disreputable hangout for world travelers. The atmosphere in the "flop house" was vile, and the hotel reeked of hashish and opium smoke. Immorality was rampant.

Although YWAM did their best to minister to these lost young people, little spiritual progress was made that first summer. Yet we all learned much from that experience.

And so the following June, a team of fifteen Youth with a Mission workers drove to Kabul from Europe. And our church rented the two top floors of a hotel located in the heart of the city. It was one of the cleaner hotels, and the atmosphere was pleasant.

In a few days, the YWAM team opened a tea room there. In these pleasant and homelike quarters, they began to minister to the starving hippies. They called it, "The Way Out."

The rules of behavior were very strict. Young people climbing the ninety-two stairs to the tea room read the regulations at the entrance: "No smoking of any kind. No immorality or bad language allowed. Anyone who does not abide by these regulations will have to leave."

God answered prayer, and many young people became Christians through this ministry. The Way Out offered hope to the desperate. YWAM also took this ministry into the prisons. The team began visiting local jails and, through their witness, God began moving among drug addicts and smugglers imprisoned there.

One German boy, after overdosing on drugs, was found wandering aimlessly about the streets of Kabul. He did not even know his name or his nationality when the Afghan police picked him up. The police could only identify him when they checked his passport in his pocket.

Although the family had offered to pay for his return trip to Germany, no airline would accept the responsibility of taking him unless a doctor or nurse was in attendance.

So The Way Out people asked permission to take him to their residence, which the police readily granted, happy to get rid of him. The young man was terribly malnourished, so he was fed with good, nutritious food.

He had also become demon-possessed through his involvement with Eastern religions, and evil spirits forced him to try to commit suicide. He once slit his wrists, and another time tried to jump from the hotel's sixth floor onto the pavement below.

Because of his mental state, a Christian young person had to stay with him 'round the clock, watching him and praying for him. One day he was finally delivered from demons and came to his senses. Then he was led to a personal faith in Jesus Christ. From that moment on, a tremendous transformation began taking place in his life day by day.

The next time the Afghan police saw him, they were incredulous. They refused to believe he was the same person! It was not until they had checked out his passport again that they were convinced.

"What happened?" they asked him. This gave him the opportunity to share with them how the power of Jesus Christ had set him free, and that by receiving Jesus as his Savior he was a new man. "If any man be in Christ, he is a new creation," he told them.

Officials in the German Embassy were utterly amazed when he walked into their offices, healed and in his right mind. They had given up on him, thinking there was no hope. When he told them about The Way Out, they sent a representative to investigate.

As the man from the Embassy walked through the two floors, meeting converts who only a short time before had been on heavy drugs—and whose faces now radiated the light of their new-found joy—he exclaimed, *"Wunderbar!* I never imagined that anything like this was possible. Why wasn't The Way Out started in Kabul long before this?"

He returned and gave a full report to the German Embassy. The Embassy then took up a voluntary offering and sent this as a contribution to the staff to help them with their ministry.

That same summer another Youth with A Mission team, headed up by Floyd and Sally McClung, witnessed as they traveled the "Hippie Trail" between Europe and Nepal. As they came back through Afghanistan the end of August, five of their team felt called to stay and continue the Kabul ministry.

They realized the need for a place where converts could be separated from their former associates in the drug culture, so they rented a house in a Kabul suburb. The new place was called *Dilaram* ("heart's peace"). The McClungs kept in close touch with our church, and thirty or forty of these young people attended our services every Sunday.

I will never forget one service in January, 1973, when eight young men and women from *Dilaram* were baptized in a single service. There was hardly a dry eye in the church as they shared their incredible testimonies.

"I saw the light of God on their faces," said one Afghan young man who attended that service.

The Youth With A Mission ministry in Kabul grew to the point that new converts, along with mature Christian young people, were sent out to establish similar work in Katmandu, Nepal, and New Delhi, India. A headquarters for the *Dilaram* ministry was also established in Amsterdam as well as on a farm in the Dutch countryside.

The Way Out helped many Afghanistan visitors escape the evil clutches of the drug culture and find new lives in Christ.

Operation Rescue

Some of our Gordon-Conwell students, staff, faculty and alumni/ae have been involved in the abortion issue. Professor Jack Davis of our Theology Department has been very active in pro-life activities and debates. Also Joe Foreman is the Assistant to Randall Terry, the founder and director of Operation Rescue. Joe graduated from Gordon College and then studied one year at Gordon-Conwell.

Many of our students and staff have been arrested as they have sought to block abortion clinics. A member of the staff, Rob Filos, has been imprisoned more than thirty times! One of our women students, Susan O'Brien, was treated very badly by the police in a rescue in Rhode Island. But in prison one woman inmate said to her, "I deserve to be here, but you are here only because you tried to save babies." And while Susan was in jail, she led this fellow prisoner to a saving knowledge of Jesus Christ.

I have not been arrested, but I have carried banners against abortion and have accompanied different people on Operation Rescue by being present for prayer.

It has been shocking to see and hear the blasphemy of those who are for abortion. Outside one clinic, I saw a well-dressed woman carrying a three-foot high crucifix of Jesus Christ on the cross all covered with condoms! Others were singing the tunes of Christian songs to vile words.

This showed me that they had some kind of church background but had rebelled and turned against the faith. One cannot help but notice the anti-Christian spirit of those outside and inside the clinics who are pro-abortion.

On the other hand, those leading the battle against abortion are often outstanding Christians. Randall Terry is a graduate of Elim Bible College, where he and his wife prepared to become missionaries in Mexico, before he started Operation Rescue. I met him at a rally in a Roman Catholic Church in the Boston area and was very impressed with his dedication, and his ability to answer the questions of the media. He is a man clearly anointed with the Holy Spirit. To hear the Catholic priests preach and pray in that rally, you would have taken them for evangelicals. Many of them openly confessed that they were born-again Christians and charismatics who manifested God's gifts.

The renewal movement of the Holy Spirit and the pro-life issue have brought the evangelical wings of the Protestant and the Catholic Churches together in common causes.

Christians need to take a stand on this issue. If we remain passive, God will surely judge our nation as well as other countries which allow and even advocate abortion. Those who do not get involved in helping the pre-born are like the two religious men Christ told about who passed by on the other side of the road when they saw the man who had fallen among thieves—without doing anything to help him. If we love our neighbor, we are to be like the good Samaritan who had pity and helped save the person's life.

Those who claim to be pro-choice make a fundamental error in logic. God has clearly commanded that we should not murder, therefore abortion is not a matter of choice. It is a sin.

The Supreme Court, since its inception, has pointed out that liberty is not the freedom to do wrong, but the freedom to do right. Committing adultery, lying, stealing and murder are not a matter of choice or liberty, but these acts break the very laws of our country, and especially the commands of God.

We are not free to do evil, but rather free to do good. The whole abortion issue seems to be summed up in the words of Jesus Christ when He said, "The thief (or Satan) only comes to steal, to kill and to destroy: but I have come that they may have life, and have it more abundantly" (John 10:10).

The Bible and Prayer in Public Schools

When the United States Supreme Court in effect took the Bible and prayer out of the public schools in the early 1960's, we were in Afghanistan.

I was so concerned about this that I wrote a personal letter to each of the nine Supreme Court Judges. I asked them why it had taken almost two hundred years to come to the conclusion that this practice was unconstitutional. I mentioned that it was obvious the Constitution had not changed, but that their interpretation of it had. I wrote that historically our public schools were founded to teach children how to read so that they could read the Bible. But now they could read almost anything except the Bible.

I went on to say I felt this was a basic misinterpretation of the separation of Church and State. The framers of our Constitution did not want the domination of one over the other, nor the opposition of one to the other, but the cooperation of one with the other. We were to render to Caesar the things that were Caesar's in relation to the State. But we were also to render to God the things that were God's in relation to the Church.

The only one who answered my letter was Justice Potter, who alone had voted against the decision of the majority.

At the time, a missionary friend from another country said to me, "You have just lost your freedom of religion in your schools in the States." He was right, in that the religion of atheistic secularism has taken over our public schools. The condition of our national educational system today with its violence, drugs and immorality shows the Biblical principle in Galatians 6:7,8 to be so true: that God cannot be mocked. Whatever people plant they will also reap. If they sow to please the sinful nature, from that they will reap destruction.

In our educational system, we have sown the wind and are reaping the whirlwind or a hurricane of violence.

It is ironic indeed that Russia, which until recently was the hub of atheistic materialism, is now introducing the Bible into their educational system—while our nation, which was founded on the Scriptures, now forbids it in our public schools.

Families Praying Together and Staying Together

God has been ever so faithful to us in answering our prayers as a family. For example, Betty and I committed each of our three children to the Lord before they were born. Then every day following, we not only prayed for them but for their future spouses, since the Lord knew who they would be. And He has done exceeding abundantly above all we have asked.

Each of our three children has married a dedicated Christian spouse, and now we not only continue to intercede for them, but are praying daily for our grandchildren, who are such a joy to us. They too are growing into men and women of God.

Some have asked Betty and me about our morning quiet times. We try to get up at five a.m. and then pray together for our families and loved ones. In Matthew 18:19, Jesus promised, "If two of you agree on earth regarding anything they ask, it will be done by My Father Who is in heaven." As a family, we can pray together with special power.

But to get up early, we have to go to bed early since it says in Psalm 127:2, "It is vain for you to rise up early, to sit up late and eat the bread of sorrows, for so He gives His beloved sleep." We then have our Bible readings alone as well as further prayer.

We also often ask the Lord to forgive our sins and shortcomings. For this we claim I John 1:9, "If we confess our sins, He is faithful and just to forgive us our sins and to cleanse us from all unrighteousness." The fact of God's grace in restoration, after our confession, is a great source of joy in the Christian life.

We have found the Gordon-Conwell Community Directory with the pictures, names, and brief descriptions of each person to be a marvelous prayer book. We remember them by name over and over again. At times we will pray that the Lord will show His good and acceptable and perfect will to each one, and that then they will obey the Lord's will. Or we pray for needs we know they have.

Many ask us whether families on the mission field should send their children home for schooling. Betty and I believe that families should stay together. This is the reason we kept our three children with us through high school. It was only when they went to Wheaton College that they left us. Even then we had them come home often during vacations.

Some Christians wonder why their children rebel. The main reason for this, I believe, is that many Christian parents think that their service for the Lord comes before their family. I believe this is a form of idolatry because their work is not the Lord. God does come first in our lives, according to the Scriptures. Then comes our family, and thirdly, our ministry, study or other responsibility.

When we keep our priorities in the right order, God blesses. Many evangelical parents do not take the time to train up a child in the way to go, and no wonder we see so many tragedies in Christian families. In I Timothy 5:8 we read, "If anyone does not provide for his own, especially for his own family, he has denied the faith and is worse than an infidel." These are very strong words. Non-Christians take care of their own families, but evangelicals often neglect to take care of theirs adequately.

Billy Graham says that Satan is concentrating on attacking Christian families today. Let us determine by God's grace as families to pray faithfully together and to stay together for His sake and for ours.

My Dad Said, "I See Jesus!"

When my wife and I were told to leave Afghanistan, the government gave us just three days to pack up and leave the country. We had a house full of belongings—our books, rugs, furniture, china, cutlery, and other things.

Instead of spending our time packing, however, we decided to leave our things with friends and use whatever time we had left to counsel and pray with the Christians we would be leaving behind.

On the day of our departure, we took nothing with us but what we could pack into our suitcases—20 kilos or 44 pounds of weight allowance for each of us.

Several days after we left Afghanistan, we were in Pakistan. There we received a long-distance telephone call from the States saying that my father was very ill. Could we come right away?

Since we had brought very little with us, we were able to pack up and leave in twenty minutes, catching the first flight out of Pakistan for the United States.

When we arrived in Los Angeles, we went directly to the retirement community where my parents were staying. There was my father—sitting in a chair on the lawn—and he welcomed us with joy.

He only lived three days after we arrived.

On the last day of his life, we were all with him—my mother, my brother, my sister, as well as Betty and myself. We noticed that he was getting weaker and finding it harder to breath. So I asked him if he wanted to sit on the edge of the bed. He said he would like to.

I sat next to him and had my arm around him. As he sat there, he looked up at the ceiling and prayed, "Lord Jesus, help me." His face then became radiant!

"I see Jesus!" he exclaimed. "I see the Lord!" None of us saw Christ, but he did. He saw the Lord in all His glory, just as Stephen did before he died, as described in Acts chapter 7.

My father then said,

> *Bless the Lord, O my soul;*
> *And all that is within me, bless His holy name!*
> *(Psalm 103:1)*

He was so excited!

Then, because he was so full of joy and relaxed, we helped him lie down on the bed. All five of us stood around him. He then said, "O come, O come, Emmanuel!" Even though it was in April, we sang this Christmas carol.

As a family, we had memorized Psalms when we were young. My mother and father would not let us eat breakfast until we had said a Psalm together. As kids, we wanted to get to the food right away, but my mother and father would insist that we first recite a Psalm. In this way, we had memorized many Psalms, and we recited them together around his bed.

Then we sang his favorite hymns. Among them was "Amazing Grace."

> *Amazing Grace, how sweet the sound,*
> *That saved a wretch like me.*
> *I once was lost, but now am found,*
> *Was blind but now I see.*

And the last stanza goes:

> *When we've been there ten thousand years,*
> *Bright shining as the sun;*
> *We've no less days to sing God's praise*
> *Than when we first begun.*

As he lay there, my father pointed to a cushion we had given to our mother. It had the words on it, "Happiness is a Grandmother." My father pointed to that and said, "Real happiness is going to be with Jesus! I'm going to be with Jesus ... today!" He was so excited because he was about to be with his Lord.

Each of us then led in prayer, thanking the Lord for our father and for all he had meant to us and to so many. Then we sang the Doxology together.

As we sang the "Amen," Dad left us ... with a smile on his face. My mother turned to me.

"Christy, wouldn't it be just like Dad to lead his own funeral?"

The next-door neighbor heard that my father had died and she rushed over to comfort us. But when she came, the house was so full of joy that she couldn't help but leave with rejoicing in her heart.

We saw the reality of eternity. Dad's grave is inscribed with the words of the Apostle Paul, "To depart to be with Christ is far better" (Philippians 1:23).

Chapter 7

God At Work At Gordon-Conwell

From Bartender to Bible Translator

Dr. Cameron Townsend, the founder of Wycliffe Bible Translators, used to say they would accept as translators anyone—from any profession—except bartenders. But he underestimated the depth of God's grace.

Mike Trainum was once a bartender. After he left that job, he and his girl friend Donna became hippies and lived together in the woods in Virginia, where they had a marijuana farm.

While waiting for the marijuana to grow, they would take long walks. On one of these walks, a dog followed them. They looked at the dog's collar, found the name of the owner, and returned the dog to him.

They found the man drunk. With a slur to his voice, he said: "I know that I should give you a reward for finding my dog. Here." And he shoved a Bible into their hands. He probably was convicted by it and wanted to get rid of it.

Mike and Donna, who were American heathens, had never read the Bible. Now that Mike had a lot of time on his hands, waiting for the marijuana to grow, he started reading the Bible from the very beginning of Genesis. He didn't know that you should start with the New Testament. And he read all the way through to Revelation.

When Mike started to read the Bible through a second time, Donna began to wonder. He usually put aside a book once he had finished it. Curious, she would pick up the Bible and start reading it herself, when Mike didn't have it.

As a result, both Mike and Donna came to a saving knowledge of Jesus Christ by reading the Bible.

It was much later, only after they had led other hippies to Christ, that they attended church for the first time. When the people in the church saw how many hippies Mike had led to Christ, they urged him to go into the ministry.

Mike and Donna didn't know much about that since they had not even gone to a justice of the peace to be married. They did not think it worth spending the money for a piece of paper just to have a wedding certificate.

Then the people of the church also urged the couple to go to Urbana, and even paid their way. Now Mike and Donna had never even heard of the Urbana Student Missionary Convention. But they went. And it was there that they ended up at the Wycliffe Bible Translators' booth. When they heard that Wycliffe sent people to live with tribes to learn their language and translate the Bible into that tongue, they volunteered to go right on the spot—since it was through reading the Scriptures that they had come to Christ. They were told, however, that they needed theological training first, and to check out some of the seminaries represented there.

That's how they came to the Gordon-Conwell booth. I don't remember this, but they told me that I prayed with them at that time. Well, they ended up coming to Gordon-Conwell.

Now they're out in the central highlands of Papua New Guinea, working with a Stone-Age tribe who were cannibals until the 1960's. Dr. Kenneth Pike calls their language one of the most complicated in the world. To explain the number "six," Mike told me, he had to use a total of eight different words.

The only electricity they have comes from solar cells. These cells power their computer and word-processor, in which they are storing all the vocabulary to build a dictionary of the language. Solar cells also power the radio which helps them keep in touch with the main center at a school in Ukarumpa.

Donna is teaching her own four children, and depends on radio contact to keep in touch with the principal and the school.

The only running water they have is in the river that runs past the huts in which they live.

Primitive as this sounds, God had prepared them during the time they lived in a shack in Virginia without electricity or plumbing.

In Mike and Donna we see the power of the Holy Spirit to transform lives. He transformed a bartender into a Bible translator. Oh, the joy they have now. Betty and I were with them for several days in Papua New Guinea, and they showed us all around.

It was such a privilege to see this family serving the Lord in the jungles of this huge South Sea Island.

One of Wycliffe's problems has been publishing the Scriptures in many different languages at a reasonable cost. Because Mike was concerned about this, the Lord woke him up early one morning with an idea. In the darkness, he had to scribble these thoughts down with a crayon the children had left on the floor.

This developed into the concept of a computer "shell." It prepares preprinted pages with pictures. All one needs to do then is reproduce and duplicate the various languages on the same format. Instead of costing several dollars for each volume, it now costs only a few cents. UNESCO of the United Nations has been so impressed with this method that they are adopting it to help supply literature reasonably in many countries.

When Uncle Cam Townsend meets Mike in heaven, he will have to admit that even a bartender can become a Bible translator!

"He Knew Me Before I Was Born"

At Gordon-Conwell, we have a young Chinese woman named Nanan Joehana, who grew up in Indonesia. She lived in a Chinese community there before coming to the States. Her parents are still Buddhists.

Before she was born, Nanan's parents went to a clinic for her mother to have an abortion. The clinic wanted about $100 for the procedure, but her father had the equivalent of only $95 with him.

"I'll bring the rest of the money later," her father said.

"No," they told him. "Unless you give us all the money now, we can't do the abortion."

Her father became angry. "Fine, then we're not going to have the abortion."

That's why Nanan is alive today.

After going to high school, Nanan came to America and studied computer engineering. She now has a Master's degree in that field.

While Nanan was studying here at a university, her Christian roommate gave her a Bible. One day, opening it to about the middle, she came to Psalm 139 and read how God knew her even before she was born. The Living Bible says that "He scheduled (programmed) each day of my life." Being a computer engineer, this really spoke to her.

"This is the God Who took care of me before I was born, when my parents wanted to have an abortion and have me killed," she said to herself. "I want this God to be my God." And she became a Christian.

Now she is studying at Gordon-Conwell and wants to serve the Lord. Her family paid for her trip home to Indonesia at Christmas in 1991. And several in her family have already come to Christ.

He Found Christ On the Assembly Line

Paulo Romiero came to Gordon-Conwell from Brazil, where he had previously prepared for the Roman Catholic priesthood.

In Brazil, witchcraft permeates much of the culture. Even Paulo's family was deeply involved in this. Until he was in his twenties, Paulo was afraid to sleep in a room alone. He had to sleep in the same room as his parents.

Then Paulo went to a Roman Catholic seminary to become a priest. But then in his final year, when he realized he didn't know the Lord personally, he was afraid to enter the priesthood. So he left seminary and found a job in an airplane factory.

Working next to him on the factory assembly line was an evangelical Christian who led Paulo to Christ.

Paulo became a wonderful evangelist, preaching on the streets in Spanish, Portuguese, and English!

Then he came to Gordon-Conwell. While he was here at seminary, he went to the Billy Graham Amsterdam '86 Conference for Evangelists. There he met Christians from Mozambique, a Portuguese-speaking country.

"We need more missionaries in Mozambique!" they told him. So Paulo introduced them to other Brazilian Christians. Since Brazilians already speak Portuguese, it was easy for them to go quickly, without the usual language training. Today many Brazilians are serving as missionaries in Mozambique.

Paulo is now back in Brazil carrying on an effective ministry, especially exposing the cults and the occult in that nation.

Don't Close the Mission!

It is such a thrill to see how God is using a Gordon-Conwell graduate named Herbert Beerens. He graduated in 1975 and went to South Africa and became a professor of New Testament in the Baptist seminary there.

At one of their annual denominational meetings, the Baptists were so thrilled with the evangelization already done in South Africa that they were going to close the mission. Well, Herbert Beerens had one of Ralph

Winter's pie-charts which showed how many unreached peoples still had not heard the Gospel. So he showed this chart at that meeting.

When the pastors saw the tremendous job that still remained, Herbert told me that tears began to flow down their cheeks. Rather than closing the mission, they decided to open a new mission to reach unreached peoples!

They asked Herbert to take on a new position and teach twelve missions courses at their seminary. They also requested his help in finding another professor of New Testament to do his former job.

Herbert and his wife Madelain, who is a medical doctor, later went to live among one of these unreached peoples groups, and planted a church there among the Yao Muslim people of Malawi.

A Jew Finds His Messiah

Jerry Feldman played the piano for a dance band. He would practice ten hours every day.

While on the circuit, Jerry and his band played at a hotel in Florida where a charismatic conference happened to be in progress. During the conference, a little twelve-year-old boy sat down at the piano where Jerry had been practicing ten hours a day, and played the piano better than Jerry! Jerry was simply amazed.

"Where does this kid get his talent?" he asked. One lady pointed to heaven.

The Apostle Paul, being a Jew, knew that it took a miracle to win Jews. He wrote in I Corinthians 1:22 that Jews require a miraculous sign while Greeks seek after wisdom.

For Jerry, it was a miracle that this twelve-year-old boy, with very little practice, could play the piano better than he could.

And so Jerry Feldman, an Orthodox Jew from New York City, began to ask questions about Jesus Christ. When he saw what Christ could do, he received Him as his Savior, and came here to Gordon-Conwell.

Jerry played the piano beautifully here—even more beautifully now that he has received Jesus as his Savior!

He graduated from Gordon-Conwell with a Master of Divinity degree and is now pastoring a Messianic synagogue.

The Apostle Paul, who was a rabbi when he received Christ as his Messiah, says in Romans 11:5, "At this present time there is a remnant according to the election by grace." It's thrilling that down through the centuries, there has been a remnant of Jewish believers who have come to know Christ as their Messiah. Many of them, like Paul, have been great scholars and talented leaders.

Two Nurses in Calcutta

We had two students at Gordon-Conwell who were registered nurses: Lynn Bolte and Harriett Whitesides. They told me in the fall of 1978 they believed God was calling them to go and work with Mother Teresa in Calcutta. This was before Mother Teresa had received the Nobel Prize.

I suggested that they make it mainly a prayer ministry.

"You won't have much opportunity to use your nursing," I said. Instead, I advised them to write down the names of everyone they met and to pray for those people as much as possible. And they did.

As they were working with Mother Teresa at the Home for the Sick and Dying, a wealthy Hindu lady came to see the work. She spoke English beautifully. They wrote down her name and prayed for her.

A few days later, Lynn and Harriett were walking across Calcutta—a city of eleven million people—to visit some children in an orphanage. The weather was so hot that they became unbearably thirsty. They stopped a woman on the street and asked her where they could get some tea to drink. Drinking water there can be dangerous.

"Wait right here," the lady said. She went into the house right by the road. Then she beckoned them inside. Lynn and Harriett entered this beautiful home and were shown into a lovely living room, where the lady had them sit down.

Who should walk into the room at that moment but the same wealthy Hindu lady who had come to Mother Teresa's a few days earlier. The very lady they had been praying for!

"I'm so glad you came to visit me," the lady said. "I've been hoping that someone from Mother Teresa's work would come." Then she served them tea, and they shared the Gospel with her.

Out of the millions of people in Calcutta, the Lord had led them straight to her home!

Now, that's a miracle. But it happened in answer to prayer.

When the Indian nuns at Mother Teresa's Sisters of Charity found out that Lynn and Harriett were students in seminary, they said, "We want to learn more about the Bible. Could you come back and teach us the Scriptures?"

When they returned here and told of their experiences, twenty-six students went to Calcutta the next summer. This started the Overseas Missions Practicum, which has continued over the years and is now headed by Dr. Gary Bekker.

God's Blessings In African Missions

Christian Relief Work

The major drought that affected much of northern Africa several years ago has also opened up other areas to ministries of mercy. One example is Mauritania.

We had two students here at Gordon-Conwell, both of whom came to the Lord as Americans in Africa. One had gone there with the Peace Corps and was hitchhiking when a missionary gave him a ride and led him to Christ. The same missionary also brought a secretary at the American Embassy to the Lord. Both young people came to Gordon-Conwell, where they fell in love and were married.

The young woman took a special course with me on Mauritania because she and her husband felt so burdened for this completely closed Muslim country. They went with a mission and studied Arabic and French before doing relief work in Mauritania. Because of the famine and drought, they came to minister to the people for whom they had been praying.

African Enterprise

African Enterprise was established by Dr. Richard Peace, Professor of Evangelism at Gordon-Conwell, and Michael Cassidy when they were both students at Fuller Seminary. They saw the need for using media to reach large numbers of people in Africa. And they have sponsored several large conferences. David Bliss also worked with them, but then came to Gordon-Conwell for further training in theology in 1974.

David started a travel agency while he was a student here. He had come to me for advice because he couldn't find a job to help support his wife Debbie and little girl Sarah.

"David," I told him, "I had to go through school completely on scholarships and part-time jobs, so I worked for a travel agency. I'm surprised they don't have one here. Why don't you start a travel agency at Gordon-Conwell? You have biblical authority that the travel industry is going to be prosperous because in Daniel 12:4 it says, 'In the last days, many will go to and fro.'"

He went to the House of Travel in South Hamilton and arranged to be their representative on campus.

Thus David was able to get a position as a travel agent, enabling him to travel anywhere in the world at a 90 percent discount. As a result, he flew all the way to Nairobi for the Pan-African Christian Leadership Assembly (PACLA), sponsored by African Enterprise, and also traveled through other parts of South Africa, South America and California before flying back to Boston—for a very low fare.

Another conference sponsored by African Enterprise was the South African Christian Leadership Assembly (SACLA), held in Johannesburg. My son Martin, after he graduated from Gordon-Conwell, went to South Africa to help David and Debbie Bliss with that conference. Since he had taken Dr. Peace's course on the use of media in evangelism, he produced a colored slide presentation on it.

Later on David and Debbie Bliss helped establish the Andrew Murray Center for Prayer for Revival and Missions in Wellington, South Africa. It was here that Andrew Murray pastored a Dutch Reformed Church for many years, establishing a base for missions. The Blisses sent out interracial South African mission teams to Mozambique and worked with refugees from that country.

Setting the Captive Free

One Sunday afternoon I received a phone call from one of our Chinese students at Gordon-Conwell.

"Would you please come immediately," he asked me. "My wife is in a terrible condition." He sounded distraught.

Although we had a guest at our home for Sunday dinner, I asked to be excused and immediately rushed to his apartment. His wife had suddenly gone into convulsions. From other information her husband gave me, I knew she was oppressed by demons.

At one time I did not believe that a Christian could have demons *(see "A 'Missionary' Is Delivered of a Demon" in Chapter 3)*. But over the years I have seen this happen many times with my own eyes, and have also witnessed their deliverance.

Another Christian friend, whom we called, joined us as we prayed and ministered together to that lady. The Lord set her free. More than thirty demons were cast out of her!

One by one, we commanded the demons, in the name of Jesus Christ, to identify themselves and come out. As each one gave its name, we would command that demon by name to release her and come out. They all came out! And the young wife was completely set free!

During the deliverance, we learned that some of these demons had entered her when she was only a little girl three years old in Hong Kong. The demons not only identified themselves but they also told us when they had entered, speaking through her voice.

Today this lady is a radiant Christian, active in her church. And God is using her in a mighty way to help others.

Unfortunately, many Christians don't realize the need for commands in the mighty power and Name of Christ for deliverance. "Let's pray for so-and-so," they'll say. But it takes more than prayer. It takes deliverance! We must speak with the authority and power given to us in the Name of Jesus Christ and command the evil spirits to come out. That's what Christ did. And the fact that 25 percent of Christ's ministry involved deliverance proves to us the importance that He Himself laid on this ministry.

"Jesus Healed Me of an Incurable Disease"

When Susan Habib entered Gordon-Conwell in the fall of 1982, she had an incurable disease, the Familial Mediterranean Fever (FMF) which she had inherited from her Phoenician ancestors in Lebanon. That semester she was sick most of the time.

First indications of this sickness had appeared when she was a student at Syracuse University. But she believed that God wanted her to go with us on the Overseas Missions Practicum the summer of 1983 to work with Afghan refugees in Pakistan. She claimed the Scripture promise in I Thessalonians 5:24, "Faithful is He Who has called you, Who also will do it." There was much intercession about this in the daily missions prayer meeting as well as in the special gatherings of the students who planned to go.

In January, she attended a Women's Aglow evening meeting in Newburyport, Massachusetts, with her mother. The woman leading the meeting had a word of knowledge from the Holy Spirit that the Lord wanted to heal someone there who had a genetic disease. She asked if there were anyone with such a need.

Susan waved her hand and was invited forward. They prayed for her, and she was completely healed!

When Susan went to her doctor, who was a Jewish Professor at Harvard Medical School as well as a specialist in internal medicine at Massachusetts General Hospital, he was amazed.

"No one is ever cured of this disease! But I cannot figure it out."

"You do not have any more symptoms!" her doctor said.

She then told him how the Lord had healed her.

After orientation for the Overseas Missions Practicum, which included rappeling down a cliff, Susan was part of the team of seven students who joined Betty and me on the trip to Pakistan. Her name was a popular one there since many people are named Habib, and one of the major financial institutions in the country is called the Habib Bank. This gave her immediate acceptance with those she met.

Also, while she was there, she became engaged to David Aune who had just graduated from Gordon-Conwell.

On the way back from Pakistan, we were able to go to the Billy Graham Conference for Evangelists in Amsterdam in the summer of 1983. It only cost $20 extra per ticket for the stopover on Pakistan International Airways.

Susan is now happily married to David and they recently returned to New England after he pastored a church in Florida. At present, they are living in Providence, Rhode Island, where he is completing his Ph.D. at Brown University in New Testament studies.

Recently, I saw Susan and asked her how she was feeling. "Wonderful!" was her answer. "My doctor is still baffled. I have had no further symptoms of the disease. And God has given us two beautiful boys!"

Goodness And Mercy

When I came to Gordon-Conwell in the fall of 1974, Michael Ford was a student here while his father was President in the White House. Because of this, he had to have two Secret Service men with him at all times. They tried to look like students, but you could easily spot them. For one thing, most of them were chain smokers. Since no one was allowed to smoke in classes, you would see them take turns rushing outside and lighting up quickly to keep from getting a nicotine fit.

Mike and his wife Gayle lived on the top floor of a house in Ipswich, while the the Secret Service rented the floor below. Since the Secret Service men were with Mike so much, he had wonderful opportunities to witness to them about the Lord Jesus Christ, even as Paul did to the Roman soldiers who were constantly with him.

Whenever Mike and Gayle would take a walk in the woods, the two men would always be seen stumbling along behind them.

This led some at Gordon-Conwell to remark that the secret service men reminded them of the Twenty-Third Psalm

> *Surely goodness and mercy will follow me*
> *all the days of my life ...*

So they nicknamed the two men "Goodness" and "Mercy"!

Chapter 8

Afghanistan's Apostle Paul

He Counted the Cost for Christ

When Betty and I went to Afghanistan in 1951 as "tentmakers" or self-supporting witnesses, we prayed that God would raise up a modern Apostle Paul from the people there. Little did we dream that the Lord would answer our prayer in the person of a young blind boy.

During 1964, a youngster whom we will call Paul enrolled in the NOOR Institute for the Blind in Kabul when he was fourteen years of age. Paul and his sister were both born with infantile glaucoma. At birth he could see, but went blind when he was a boy of five.

His blindness had come from a religious custom formerly practiced in Afghanistan which often led to first cousins marrying. Because women were heavily veiled, a couple were not allowed to see each other until after the wedding ceremony had been performed. Then a mirror would be placed before them and the bride's veil would be lifted and they would see each other face to face for the first time.

Many did not want to take this chance. Instead they married first cousins, since they had seen each other in their homes because their mothers and fathers were brothers and sisters. But this often resulted in mental and physical handicaps.

Even with this handicap, Paul was probably the most brilliant person I have ever met. At fourteen, he had already memorized the whole Koran in its original language. It would be like an English speaker learning the complete New Testament by heart in Greek, since Arabic was not Paul's mother tongue. He completed the six primary grades of the Institute for the Blind in three years.

While taking his classes in Braille, Paul also mastered English. He did this by listening and repeating what he heard on broadcasts over a transistor radio. With the help of a small ear plug, he would tune in programs in English coming into Afghanistan from other countries. He then started asking questions about what he had heard, such as, "What do you mean by substitutionary atonement?" He had heard such theological concepts on Christian radio broadcasts like the Voice of the Gospel coming from Addis Ababa in Ethiopia.

Finally, he shared with Betty that he had received Jesus Christ as his personal Savior through listening to these programs. She asked him if he realized he could be killed for this, since the Islamic law of apostasy dictates death for anyone leaving that religion. He answered, "I have counted the cost and am willing to die for Christ, since He already died on the cross for me."

Paul then became the spiritual leader of the Afghan Christians. In the Institute for the Blind in Kabul, the students elected him as the president of their association. But the next year, after it became known that he had become a Christian, he lost the election for this position. Betty told him how sorry she was that he had lost. He replied by quoting what John the Baptist said of Jesus, "He must increase, and I must decrease" (John 3:30). His goal in life was not to seek prominence for himself, but to be a humble servant of his Lord.

Paul's father said that before he had entered the Institute for the Blind, he had been like a cold piece of unlit charcoal. But after his experience there, he had become like a red hot burning ember.

Once he came to see me and asked to borrow an English Braille copy of the Gospel of John. He opened it and read with his fingers. Then he returned it and said that his question had been answered. I asked him what his question was. He replied that in John 14:34, Jesus said, "A new commandment I give you that you love one another." He had wondered why the Lord had called it "new," since the commandment to "love your neighbor as yourself" had already been given by God to Moses over a millennium before, as recorded in the Old Testament book of Leviticus 19:18. But now he understood.

I asked him to tell me. He explained that until the time of Christ's incarnation, the world had never before actually seen love personified. He went on to state that the Bible reveals that God is love, and that Jesus as God in human flesh was Love Incarnate. This was what made the commandment new. Jesus said, "A new commandment I give you that you love one another as I have loved you." In His perfect life, Jesus has not only given us a new model of love to follow, but He also indwells us by His Holy Spirit and therefore He bears the fruit of love through us!

Paul was the first blind person to attend regular public schools in Afghanistan along with the sighted students. There he had a small tape recorder on which he took down everything his teachers said, so he could listen to the lessons again and again and master them thoroughly. In this way he became the number one student out of hundreds at his grade level.

Those who failed in their classes were given a second chance to take examinations at the end of the three-month vacation. Paul studied the next year's courses during the break and then passed the tests with the students who had failed. In this way he went through high school in record time, finishing two grades each year.

At Christmas in Kabul, we used to have an outdoor pageant under lights in the garden of the house church where we lived. This included a live donkey, cows, sheep and hybrid Bactrian camels. As hundreds of Afghans came to see the story of Christmas for the first time, Paul narrated it over the public address system in their Dari language.

He also would come to see me in order to study Calvin's *Institutes*, since he wanted to grasp the Biblical concepts of this great Reformation leader.

Paul fell in love with an Afghan girl who was legally blind and was studying in the Institute. After a courtship, they decided they wanted to get married. As far as we know, this was the first Christian wedding between two Afghan Muslim converts ever held in that nation.

He told me that he also wanted to study Islamic Law so that he could defend Christians who might be persecuted for their faith. He therefore entered the University of Kabul, from which he successfully graduated with his law degree.

The Christoffel Mission to the Blind in Germany gave the Institute in Afghanistan an extensive library of Braille books in German. Since Paul wanted to read these, along with his other classes, he went to the Goethe Institute in Kabul and learned German. As the top student there too, he won a scholarship to go to Germany to study advanced German. When the representatives found out that he was blind, they said they would have to give the scholarship to the second student since they did not have accommodations for a person who could not see. He asked them what he would have to do. They replied that he would have to travel alone and take care of himself. He said that he could do that. Therefore they finally accepted him. While studying there with top students from Goethe Institutes from around the world, he was number one in this advanced course as well!

He also traveled to Saudi Arabia where he entered a memory contest on the Koran. He took first place in the competition there! The Saudi Muslim judges were so chagrined that a non-Arabic speaker had won that they had to figure out some way to keep from losing face. They finally decided to award two gold medals: one to the best Arab, and the other to the best non-Arab.

Paul, along with a talented and dedicated Finnish woman missionary, also translated the New Testament from Iranian Persian into his own Dari dialect. This was published by the Pakistan Bible Society in Lahore. Its third edition was put out by Cambridge University Press in England in 1989, and is the translation distributed to Afghans all around the world.

Because numerous blind students like Paul had become Christians, in March 1973, as already mentioned, the Muslim government in Afghanistan sent a written order closing the two Institutes for the Blind, the one in Kabul, with more than a hundred pupils, and the other in Herat, with more than forty.

Betty and I were ordered out of the country in three days, after we had served there for twenty-two years. All expatriate teachers of the blind, along with their families, were forced to leave Afghanistan within one week.

The destruction of the church building in Kabul

The Muslim government then destroyed the Christian Church building in Kabul, after they had once given permission to build it. *(For the story on building the church, see "Jesus Said, 'I Will Build My Church'" in Chapter 6.)*

When troops arrived and started knocking down the wall between the street and the Church property prior to destroying it, a German Christian businessman, Hans Mohr—who purchased most of the semi-precious lapis lazuli stone mined each year in Afghanistan—went to see the Mayor of Kabul to see if he could get him to rescind the order he had given.

The mayor had been educated in Germany.

Mr. Mohr said to the mayor:

"If your Government touches that House of God, God will overthrow your Government!"

This proved to be a prophetic word.

The mayor then sent a letter to the congregation ordering them to give over the Church for destruction. That way the Government would not have to pay compensation.

The congregation replied that they could not give the church to anyone, since it did not belong to them. It had been dedicated to God.

They also added that if the Government took it and destroyed it, the officials would be answerable to God.

Soldiers, police, workmen and bulldozers were then sent to destroy the Church. The congregation, instead of opposing them, offered them tea and cookies. Christians all around the world prayed and many wrote letters to Afghan Embassies in various countries. Billy Graham and other Christian leaders signed a statement of concern and sent it to King Zahir Shah.

The Afghan Government received a secret police report that there was an "underground church" in Afghanistan. Since they did not understand this term, they dug twelve feet below the foundation looking for the underground church!

On July 17, 1973, the Muslims completely destroyed the Church building and finished digging up the foundation.

That very night, the Afghanistan Government was overthrown in a coup!

Afghans, who are quick to see omens in events, say that Jesus Christ came down from heaven and overthrew the Government because it had overthrown His Church. It had been a monarchy for 227 years. That night it became a Republic under President Daoud. Then in 1978 the Republic was toppled by a Communist coup, followed by the Russian invasion just after Christmas in 1979. Millions of Afghans had to flee their country as refugees. One of them said to me, "Ever since our Government destroyed that Christian Church, God has been judging our country."

Under the Communists, the Institute for the Blind in Kabul was reopened and Paul was put in charge. He did a fine job in reorganizing it. He also took his Master's degree in Education at the University of Kabul by producing the first system of shorthand for Dari Braille in Afghanistan.

Since he served as President of Handicapped Education for the nation, he was an official under the Communist régime and pressure was brought on him to join the party. But he refused. One official told him that if he did not join, he might be killed. He replied that he was not afraid of that since he was ready to die. He then asked the Communist if he were prepared to die.

Finally Paul was arrested under false charges and put in the Puli Charkhi political prison outside Kabul where tens of thousands were executed. There was no heat in the jail to protect the prisoners from the cold winter weather. He had to sleep on the freezing mud floor with only his overcoat. A prisoner next to him was shaking with cold since he did not even have a jacket.

Paul knew that John the Baptist had said, "The man who has two coats should share with him who has none" (Luke 3:11). But he took off his only coat and gave it to his neighbor. From then on, the Lord miraculously kept him warm every night. He slept as if he had a comforter over him.

In prison, the Communists gave Paul shock treatments to try to brainwash him. The electric burns from these left scars on his head. But they could not break his spirit with this cruel psychological treatment aimed at destroying his mind. He was then offered a chance to study Russian in prison. There he mastered this language as well. The Communists finally freed him in December 1985.

Following his release from prison, Paul read Genesis 12:1-3 in his English Braille Bible, "The Lord said to Abram, 'Leave your country, your people and your father's household and go to the land I will show you. I ... will bless you ... and you will be a blessing. I will bless those who bless you, and whoever curses you, I will curse; and all peoples on earth will be blessed through you.'"

He felt God was calling him to leave Afghanistan and go to Pakistan as a missionary. He therefore got in touch with a friend who was a blind beggar. Then he dressed himself in rags. On their way out of the country, he let his friend do all the talking. They thus were able to get through the Soviet check points along the main highway from Kabul. It took them twelve days to travel the 150 miles to the Khyber Pass and then on into Pakistan.

After Paul arrived in Peshawar, he typed us a beautiful letter saying that he had reached there safely. I answered and invited him to come to Gordon-Conwell Theological Seminary to study Hebrew since he was then working on a translation of the Old Testament into Dari. He said he would love to come, but that he had too much to do among the Afghans and Pakistanis.

Paul's wife and their three daughters joined him in Pakistan, where he started schools for the blind in the refugee camps. He also learned Urdu and preached in the churches in Pakistan. Then he completed a book of Bible stories for children in Dari.

In a prophetic word, Paul once told a Canadian Christian friend that if Gulbuddin Hikmatyar, the leader of the fanatical Muslim group called Hisbe Islami (the Party of Islam), captured him, he would be killed. They were both students at the University of Kabul at the same time, Paul was studying law and Gulbuddin was studying engineering. So they knew each other. It was probably there that Gulbuddin learned Paul was a Christian.

On March 23, 1988, Paul was kidnapped by this group and accused of being a CIA agent because he knew English, a KGB or Khad spy because he knew Russian, and an apostate from Islam because he was a Christian. He was beaten for hours with rods. A sighted person can brace and flinch when the blow comes. But one who is blind cannot see the club coming and thus gets the full force, even like the torture the Lord Jesus Christ experienced when He was blindfolded and struck (Luke 22:64).

When I heard of his capture, I went to Pakistan in the summer of 1988 to see if I could help secure his release. I talked with officials there, but all their attempts to free him failed. He apparently was taken out of Pakistan and held in a prison inside Afghanistan. I met with his wife and their three daughters. Four months after Paul's capture, his wife had a beautiful boy who looks like his father. No one knows whether Paul ever heard that he had a son.

The latest word is that the Hisbe Islami party cruelly and painfully murdered him. This same group caught and tortured two Pakistani Christians who were taking relief items to needy Afghans. Before releasing them, their captors said, "We are not going to kill you the way we did Paul. But don't let us catch you doing this again."

In addition, an Afghan news reporter in Peshawar claims to have evidence that Hisbe Islami murdered Paul in a very barbaric way. Also the Pakistani government official in charge of refugee affairs for the Northwest Frontier Province admitted that an Afghan had been killed for becoming a Christian.

When Betty and I were back in Kabul for three weeks in the spring of 1991, an Afghan friend told us this story. He too had been captured for his faith and put into prison. But in the fighting between rival factions, a rocket hit and destroyed the building where he was being held. His guards ran for cover. And he walked out of the jail unharmed. This seems like a replay of the miraculous deliverance of the apostles from prisons in Acts chapters 4, 12 and 16. This Afghan Christian then told us that friends who did not know that he was a believer had confided in him that Paul had been murdered for his faith in Jesus Christ.

The United Nations Universal Declaration of Human Rights in article 13 states, "Everyone shall have the right to freedom of thought, conscience and religion; freedom to manifest one's religion or belief." Paul's experience is clearly an infringement of these human rights. He was denied these rightful freedoms and, as far as we know, has been martyred for his faith.

God does not force a belief system upon people. He has given them the liberty to choose. Therefore what right does an earthly régime or group have to impose a certain belief system?

Our prayer is that in the future Afghanistan will respect the freedom of religion which is basic to all other liberties.

There is a popular Dari Afghan proverb which substantiates this truth as it states, "Isa'i ba dini khud, Musa'i ba dini khud." Translated it means, "Let the followers of Jesus practice their religion, and the followers of Moses theirs."

Before his capture, Paul asked a Christian friend, Arley Loewen, whether he would take care of his family if anything happened to him. The friend said he would, not realizing that a short time later Paul would be kidnapped. He was able to arrange for Paul's wife and the two younger children to come to North America.

Jesus prophesied, "A time is coming when anyone who kills you will think he is offering service to God" (John 16:2). After His resurrection, He commanded His followers, "Be faithful, even unto death, and I will give you the crown of eternal life" (Revelation 2:10). If Paul has been martyred for Christ, as many sources seem to indicate, he has gone to his eternal reward. And all of us of like precious faith will one day see him again.

The Bible promises, "We who are still alive and are left will be caught up together with them in the clouds to meet the Lord in the air. And so shall we (along with Paul) ever be with the Lord" (I Thessalonians 4:17). Then we will be able to learn the full story of his dedicated life.

He counted the cost and willingly offered himself up for Christ Who had loved him and given Himself up for him.

Index

A

Abraham . . . . 7 - 10
African Enterprise . . . . 165 - 166
Alford, Michael 116
Anas, Mohammed 125
Antablin, Bill 131
Armstrong, Neil 30
Aune, David 168

B

Baqui, Hajji Yahya . . . . 96 - 97
Barendsen, Erik and Eeva . . . . . . 100 - 101
Barrett, David 102
Beerens, Herbert and Madelain . . . . 162 - 163
Bekker, Gary 164
Bell, Clayton 70
Bibles for the World 92
BINA, Blind Institute of Noor in
   Afghanistan 126, 170
Birch, John . . . . 73 - 76
Bliss, David and Debbie . . . . . . 86, 165 - 166
Bolte, Lynn 164
Branch, Bob 141
Brydon, Dr. 65

C

Cable, Mildred 24
Cain, Paul 144
Cameron, Jim 150
Cantine, James . . . . 106 - 107
Carmichael, Amy 82
Carter, President Jimmy . . . . 62 - 63
Cassidy, Michael 165
Ceausescu, President . . . . 58 - 59
Chennault, General Claire . . . . 74 - 75
Christoffel Mission to the Blind 31, 125 - 126, 171
Christoffel, Pastor . . . . 31 - 32
Christy, Dr. Norval 134
Clark, Dennis 131
Clark, Greg 141
Cooley, Robert 132
Cowan, Leonard 141
Cromwell, Oliver 104
Cudney, Jim and Margaret 17

D

Daoud, President 173
Davidson, Flora 99, 114
Davis, Jack 132, 153
de Mayer, Jenny 106
Dewey, John 135

Doolittle, Colonel Jimmy . . . . 73 - 74
du Plessis, David 88

E

Eisenhower, President Dwight D. 121
Eliot, John . . . . 103 - 105
Elliot, Elisabeth 123
Elson, Edward 121
Emery, James 101
En-lai, Chou 127
Ensor, John and Kristen 61
Evangelism Explosion 148

F

Feldman, Jerry 163
Filos, Rob 153
Finney, Charles 79
Fleming, Dr. and Mrs. Robert (Bertha) 85
Ford, Michael and Gayle 168
Foreman, Joe 153
Franklin, Benjamin 83

G

Gantt, Dwyatt . . . . 59 - 60
Glasser, Arthur 61
Gordon, Adoniram Judson 54, 136, 148
Gospel Recordings . . . . 15 - 17
Graham, Billy . . . . 17 - 19, 45,
   . . . . 70 - 71, 147 - 149, 173
Graham, Rosa 70
Graham, Ruth 70, 149, 156
Graham, Virginia 70
Grant, Isobel 124
Gregory the Illuminator . . . . 87 - 88

H

Habib, Susan . . . . 167 - 168
Hafizullah 100
Hailson, Donna and Gene . . . . 44 - 45
Halladay, Lloyd . . . . 94 - 95
Ham, Rev. . . . . 68 - 69
Harper, Dr. Howard . . . . 126, 134 - 135
Harper, Monika 125
Haughey, Thomas 121
Hawthorne, Nathaniel 104
Hikmatyar, Gulbuddin 174
Hisbe Islami . . . . 174 - 175
Holland, Sir Henry 99
Howard, David 123
Howard, Philip 123
Hunter, Ed . . . . 25 - 26
Hussein . . . . 94 - 96

I

International Afghan Mission . . . 126, 133 - 135
InterVarsity . . . . . 2, 48, 76 - 77, 114, 134, 146

J

Joehana, Nanan . . . . 161 - 162
Johnson, T.Y. 113
Jones, Clarence 47

K

Kahn, Dilawar 97
Kai-shek, Madame Chiang 69
Karim, Qazi Abdul 99
Keh, Kinston . . . . 54, 127 - 130
Keller, Helen 125
Kennedy, James 148
Khan, Jahan . . . . 97 - 99
Khan, Nasrullah 100
Khan, Saeed . . . . 11 - 12
Kharlov, George 62
Khoubiar, Stephan 2
Khomeini, Ayatollah 13, 15, 33, 62
Kinsler, Ross 101
Knowland, Senator William 75
Konuk, Farouk . . . . 18 - 19
Kuhlman, Kathryn . . . . 137 - 139

L

Lambie, Dr. Thomas 102
Lamont, Robert 138
Latin America Mission 123
Laubach, Dr. 116
Lausanne Congress 68, 93, 123
Leitch, Addison 146
Liddell, Eric 62, 76
Livingstone, David . . . . 80 - 82
Loewen, Arley 176
Lovelace, Richard 56

M

Magney, Gordon and Grace 63
Maracle, John . . . . 104 - 105
Massoud, General 66
Mather, Cotton 103
Mazzafar 100
McClung, Floyd and Sally 152
McGavran, Donald A. 18
McGinn, Sam and Linda 149
Mekeel, Herbert . . . . 115 - 116, 143
Miller, William 35, 99, 123
Mission Aviation Fellowship 64
Mitchell, Hubert 147
Mitchell, Mrs. 40
Moffat, Robert 80
Mohammed, Hajji Sultan 31
Mohammed, the Prophet . 26, 33, 53, 89 - 90, 94
Mohdullah . . . . 124 - 125
Mohr, Hans 172
Moody, Dwight L. . . . . 78 - 79, 121, 136
Mooneyham, Stanley 64
Moonies (Unification Church) 56
Moravians 79
Morris, Johnny . . . . 124 - 125
Morrison, Robert 80
Morrison-Knutsen Company . . . 26, 112 - 113
Mother Teresa 164
Muir, Marlene 16
Murray, Andrew 166

N

Newbrander, Nancy (Wilson) 32, 111
Nielsen, Carl . . . . 89 - 91
NOOR 100, 126

O

O'Brien, Susan 153
Ockenga, Harold J. . . . . 70 - 71, 90 - 91
Osborne, T. L. 23
OXFAM 126

P

Payne, Skip . . . . 4 - 5
Peace, Richard . . . . 165 - 166
Pennell, Dr. Theodore . . . . 97 - 99
Pfander, Dr. Karl . . . . 96 - 97
Pierce, Bob 19, 28, 82, 91
Pierson, Arthur T. 136
Pike, Kenneth 160
Potter, Supreme Court Justice 154
Pudaite, Rochunga and Mawii . . . . . 91 - 92

R

Rasmussen, Maria 99
Rees, Paul . . . . 28 - 29
Richardson, Don 53
Ridderhof, Joy . . . . 15 - 17
Ringer, Jack . . . . 134 - 135
Ritchie, Mark and Winnie 63
Roberts, Evan 2
Rogers, Jim and Jan 150
Romiero, Paulo 162
Rosser, Russell 142

S

Sang, Mansur . . . . 21 - 23
Scott, Waldron 25
SERVE 10, 64
Shafiq, Musa 126
Sherwood, Ann 16
Shook, Cleo . . . . 63 - 64
Singh, Bakht . . . . 45 - 49
Soong, Charles . . . . 62, 69 - 70
Soong, Madame (wife of Sun Yat-sen) . . 69 - 70
Soong, T.V. 70
Stegen, Erlo 86
Strachan, John . . . . 38 - 39
Student Volunteer Movement . . . 107, 136, 146
Subhan . . . . 20 - 21
Sudan Interior Mission (S.I.M.) 102

T

Tafti, Hassan Dehqani . . . . 12 - 15
ten Boom, Betsie 68
ten Boom, Corrie 68

Index 179

Terry, Randall 153
Tokos, Lazlo 59
Townsend, Cameron 159, 161
Trainum, Mike and Donna . . . . . . 159 - 161
Trotman, Dawson 132
Tson, Josef . . . . 57 - 59

U

United Mission of Nepal 85, 133
United Nations . . . 54, 119, 121, 128, 161, 175
U.S. State Department . . . . 62, 118 - 119
U.S. Supreme Court . . . . 154 - 155
Urbana Student Missionary Convention . . 101,
. . . . 136, 160

V

Van Ness, John 84

W

Walters, Gwyn . . . . 1 - 2
Ward, Larry . . . . 28 - 29
Webster-Smith, Irene . . . . 76 - 78
Werner, Hans 125
Weston, Rosemary 63
Whitefield, George . . . . 83 - 84
Whitesides, Harriett 164
Wiesinger, Pastor Sigfried 31, 125
Wilder, Robert 107, 146
Wilkerson, David 150

Wilson, Betty . . . . 8, 10, 17, 48, 63, 67 - 68, 80
. . . . 86, 111 - 119, 124 - 126,
. . . . 139 - 145, 156 - 157, 167 - 170, 172, 175
Wilson, Chris 9, 111
Wilson, J.Christy, Sr. . . . 2, 31, 105, 116 - 117,
. . . . 122 - 123, 136, 142, 156 - 158
Wilson, Martin 111, 166
Wilson, Stanley 55, 157
Wimber, John . . . . 139 - 141
Winter, Ralph 101, 163
Woodberry, Dudley 90
Woolmer, Bishop 134
World Concern 10, 63
World Evangelical Fellowship 25, 123
World Vision . . . 19, 28 - 29, 64, 77, 82 - 83, 91
Wycliffe Bible Translators . . . . 159 - 161

Y

Yandell, Barbara 61
Youth With A Mission . . . . 150 - 152

Z

Zahir Shah, His Majesty 122, 173
Zwemer, Amy 105
Zwemer, Peter . . . . 107 - 108
Zwemer, Samuel . . . . . . 17, 36, 51, 105 - 108